"When you're finally tired of best, you're ready to learn about ~~g~~ ~~~~ ~~~~, ~~~~ ~~easy~~ way and the only way. That's when you need to visit with my friend Larry Hall. With his great sense of humor and deep compassion, Larry is a friend of the seeker and an entertaining companion for those of us wishing not just to survive, but to thrive and to find God's glory in abundance. Read and enjoy your Lord and what he wants you to become!"

Jane Gibson,
artist, educator, writer of *Teacher, Here's My Heart* and *The Gracedhearts Series*

"I am thrilled to find someone asking the right question! It is not, 'What would Jesus do?' but, 'What is Jesus doing?' Larry Hall's style is engaging, and his use of his counseling background makes this a very practical and enjoyable read."

Dr. John O. York,
co-author of *The Jesus Proposal*

"...hones in on what I call a 'bull's-eye theology.' I love the emphasis on the Christ and the cross-centered nature of the gospel...powerful, personal and practical."

Dr. Paul Faulkner,
Founder, Resources for Living

"Hall proposes a new Christian mysticism—but with a difference. He grounds discipleships in seeing life in terms of worship and the experience of Christ, but he also grounds it in searching revealed truth and submitting self and life to that truth. Hall is an excellent story-teller. He paints scenes beautifully... *No Longer I* is an excellent examination of the life God desires for his people."

Dr. Perry L. Stepp in *Leaven Quarterly*

"This volume is very well written and very readable. From beginning to end, the book offers encouragement for the individual Christian to become more like Christ."

Sellers S. Crain, Jr. in *Gospel Advocate*

"Larry Hall is a change agent who is trying to re-mold the church from within—one of us at a time. How can there not be success when it is no longer I, but Christ living in me?"

F. LaGard Smith, compiler,
The Narrated Bible

"This book cuts to the heart of our life's walk—making Christ the focus rather than ourselves. Fortunately, I not only get to read the book, I get to see it lived by Larry Hall every day.

Raymond Chapman,
shepherd, Belton Church of Christ and
founder of Chapman Design Studio.

NO LONGER I

A Life Transformed

L. E. Hall

WESTBOW
P R E S S
A DIVISION OF THOMAS NELSON

Special editorial and design work by Jane Montgomery Gibson

Scripture quotations designated NCV are from the New Century Version, copyright © 1987, 1988, 1991 by Word Publishing. Used by permission.

Scripture quotations designated NIV are from The Holy Bible New International Version, copyright © 1973, 1978, 1984 by International Bible Society. Used by permission of Zondervan Bible Publishers.

Scripture quotations designated NRSV are from the New Revised Standard Version Bible, copyright © 1989, 1988, 1991 by the Division of Christian Education of the National Council of Churches of Christ in the U.S.A. Used by permission. All rights reserved.

Scripture quotations designated Phillips are from the New Testament in Modern English by J. B. Phillips, published by the Macmillan Company, copyright © 1958, 1960, 1972 by J. B. Phillips.

Scripture quotations designated RSV are from the Holy Bible, Revised Standard Version Bible, copyright © 1946, 1952 by the Division of Christian Education of the National Council of Churches of Christ in the U.S.A. Used by permission. All rights reserved.

WestBow Press books may be ordered through booksellers or by contacting:
WestBow Press
A Division of Thomas Nelson
1663 Liberty Drive
Bloomington, IN 47403
www.westbowpress.com
1-(866) 928-1240

Because of the dynamic nature of the Internet, any web addresses or links contained in this book may have changed since publication and may no longer be valid. The views expressed in this work are solely those of the author and do not necessarily reflect the views of the publisher, and the publisher hereby disclaims any responsibility for them.

Any people depicted in stock imagery provided by Thinkstock are models, and such images are being used for illustrative purposes only.

Certain stock imagery © Thinkstock.

ISBN: 978-1-4497-1940-1 (sc)
ISBN: 978-1-4497-1942-5 (hc)
ISBN: 978-1-4497-1941-8 (e)

Library of Congress Control Number: 2011932237

Printed in the United States of America
WestBow Press rev. date: 7/19/2011

FOREWORD

Jesus said, "Blessed are those who hunger and thirst for righteousness, for they will be filled." The Apostle Paul said, "... and what you have heard from me through many witnesses entrust to faithful people who will be able to teach others as well."

For anyone who hungers and thirsts for purpose and meaning in their life, Larry Hall is an experienced sage able to guide them to the table and fountainhead. He makes no claims as a pioneer, acknowledging some of those who taught and guided him to the source of spirituality.

In the prologue, Larry's description of the exchange between Jesus and the disciples reads like an eyewitness report. The remainder of the book demonstrates that Larry has spent considerable time reflecting on the words of Jesus. That time was well spent and led him to discover the crux of Jesus' message. Larry also knows what happens when that message is or is not put into practice.

One of the things I love about Larry is that he never takes himself too seriously. It is refreshing to find someone with Larry's abilities remain so unassuming about himself.

Don't allow Larry's sly humor which comes out often in the book let you underestimate his keen intelligence, knowledge, and wisdom.

Years of experience as a Christian counselor, church minister, college instructor, husband, and father are drawn together in *No Longer I*. Larry knows the Bible and the One lifted up in its pages. He is well read in the fields of psychology and theology. His knowledge from those different areas is integrated into a coherent view of life.

As one who knows the hunger and thirst for righteousness, I was blessed by this book. Following Larry as my guide I was reminded of a number of familiar sights, then some other familiar things were seen in a new light, and there were other things that I would have overlooked without Larry's observant eye.

From beginning to end Larry unpacks the meaning of what he designates to be Jesus' signature statement. Chapter after chapter I kept thinking of G. K. Chesterton's line, "Christianity has not been tried and found wanting; it has been found difficult and not tried." Larry does not understate the difficulty of the Christian life, but he also affirms that God is all powerful and provides everything we lack.

Larry carefully demonstrates that he has experienced the brokenness and witnessed the tragic dimensions of our fallen human state. But, most of all, he guides us to celebrate the transformation Jesus promises and provides in those broken and tragic moments.

I hope you find as much nourishment and refreshment as I did when reading *No Longer I*. Larry graciously shares with us the feast and refreshment he found at the table and the fountain provided by a gracious God and loving Savior.

Stan Reid, President
Austin Graduate School of Theology

SPECIAL NOTE TO THE READER

To enhance your reading of *No Longer I,* an extensive Study Guide is included at the end of the book. There are questions that introduce and prepare you for each of the book's five major sections, followed by questions that specifically cover each chapter. If you choose to use the guide, you will want to refer to it before starting each section, as well as after finishing each chapter. In the introduction to the Study Guide, you will find more helpful information and ideas on how to use it to the greatest benefit.

To
the memory of
my parents
T. H. and Mary Hall
for allowing me to search through it

To
my wife
Janet Stell Hall
for allowing me to walk through it with her

And to
my children
David Hall and Beth Hall Phillips
for allowing me to see how to get to it sooner and better

ACKNOWLEDGMENTS

Nothing in this book is original. At least it isn't meant to be. If there is any fundamental originality, I apologize. I was hoping, of course, to have said things in fresh ways; different phrasings and metaphors often bring deeper understanding, renewed appreciation, possibly even new conviction. But the message is mine only as much as it has become my story, and yours, and all the Christians' who have lived before us. This book is about what Lewis (and before him, Baxter) called "mere" Christianity. It is an attempt to capture the essence, the heart of Christian discipleship. It avoids most ancilliary subjects and areas of speculation. These may be quite worthy of discussion by others better qualified but even these discussions, to remain valid, must come back to the essential matrix. Our most fundamental touchstones must be clearly identified and passionately embraced or we will go off on numberless dead end tangents.

I must further disavow originality as I reflect on my indebtedness to so many who have had parts in bringing this book into existence. Some four decades have passed since I first realized that this book needed to be written. God, if not I, knew just how unequal to the task I was. First, he would have to fill my life with people, experiences and humblings. Then when I finally and fully accepted my ineptness and unfitness for the undertaking, he said, "Good. Now write."

In the meantime he had introduced me, in person or in print, to many wonderful people to whom and for whom I now give glad thanks. He had first laid the groundwork through saints like Dr. Anthony Lee Ash. Tony did me many favors, not the least of which was teaching me in no uncertain terms that college Bible was not just graduate Sunday School. His teaching on weekdays and his preaching on Sundays were of inmeasurable influence. Tony introduced me to the writings of C. S. Lewis who, after all these years, is still my favorite author.

Reading of Lewis in combination with the works of Dietrich Bonhoeffer and John Stott soon inspired my earliest thoughts on the main premise of this book. Over the years, those thoughts took the form of sermons, workshops and retreats, youth rallies, counseling methods, and yes, various attempts at writing. Indeed, the theme of this book has been the hinge pin of all my ministries.

So there are innumerable (and most unnamable) people to thank for suffering through efforts to get to this point. Many have even condescended to read rough manuscripts and make recommendations. Over the years, I have been blessed to co-minister along side several brilliant and godly men. Four in particular whose knowledge and insight were especially helpful during the writing process are Doctors Michael Armour, John York and John Roberts, and beloved brother Kyle Bolton. [And in this twelfth anniversary revision, I want to thank two more men of God who have been so supportive of the book and so encouraging to me as I weighed the decision to produce this edition. Thank you, more than you know, Joe Baisden and Jim Woodroof.]

Though various parts of this book have found their ways into countless classes, there are two groups in particular that were wonderfully willing guinea pigs who were subjected to the entire work as it neared completion. The feedback of the Wednesday night classes at the Western Hills Church and the Belton Church was invaluable. I am still in wonder of all the different angles, insights and questions that can surround a single paragraph.

Linnie Middleton, Aloha Nelson, Pam Bonneau, Ora Beth Royal and especially Penny Sartin did so much more than proofread, copy and collate. They provided encouragement, patience, support and some very important input on word choices.

God provided two very special people for the final polishing of the manuscript. Two outstanding writers themselves, Jane Gibson and Thom Lemmons invested far more careful attention to this work than I had any right to expect. Already juggling her responsibilities as professor, photographer, community volunteer, and homemaker with work on her own manuscript, Jane, nonetheless, embraced this work with selfless passion. Whenever I was weary of the whole process, she found just the right way to remind me that this is "a God thing." One inspired sentence from her in the margin could result in a whole page of improvements. And it can be so reassuring to know that someone else on the planet has the same, uhmm, *baroque* thought patterns. [With this second edition, I again, find myself overwhelmed with the abundance of time, talent and encouragement Jane gave so generously to this revision. I cannot imagine how it would ever have been completed without her partnership in the project.]

Though he is an extremely busy publisher and editor, Thom made me feel as if this were his most important project. He is the ideally balanced editor: He does pore carefully over each sentence with a keen eye for what will and will not read well, what needs more, what needs less. Yet, he does this with the utmost respect for the author and his style. His instructions sound more like the request, "Tell me more," than the order, "Say it my way."

Finally, I want most to thank the woman who has stood by me for thirty [now over 42] years—during most of which she kept hearing about this book that I would someday write. If she ever doubted, she did not say so. These last three years especially, the project has taken time that belonged to her, and much credit for the finished product belongs to her as well. Thank you, Janet. Your inspiration, patience, loyalty and unconditional love are blessings for which I, were I to write one hundred books, could never find adequate words of gratitude.

CONTENTS

PART ONE

The Cross
of
Christ

PROLOGUE

"Satan!"

He just called you Satan! Feeling your ears heat up and your forehead moisten, you know that once again your own reddening face has betrayed you even before you can identify the emotion. Is it embarrassment? Hurt? Anger? He probably knows. He always knows...

So many things have been racing through your mind today. For over two years now you have been taken on a ride so filled with twists and turns, ups and downs that at times you feel absolutely breathless. You've actually seen miracles. Not the seedy tricks of so-called sorcerers, not the frantic spectacles of would-be exorcists, not even the extraordinary but still natural occurrences so often called miracles. No, you have witnessed divine wonders: storms calmed with a word, multitudes fed with a boy's lunch, the dead raised with the touch of a hand. You've lost count of all the healings but each time you witness another, you see again your mother-in-law, one moment bedfast and burning with fever, the next moment healthy and playing the hostess. And that walk on the water—how can you ever describe how that felt?

Then there are his words. You've never heard such words before. Winsome words, shocking words; comforting words, affronting words; words that have cut to your heart, words that have healed your deepest wounds. But what are you to make of these words you've just heard?

It's all been so unsettling. Here you are, much too far north of Galilee for your comfort. Sure, it's beautiful here with the lush vegetation and Mount Hermon overtaking the horizon. Yes, the crowds have grown smaller and you had been afraid that they were getting out of control. And, yes, you do feel safer here near Caesarea Philippi, out of the jurisdiction of

Herod Antipas. But the region is filled with gentiles. Why did you have to come here to the outskirts of such a gaudy pagan city? The birthplace of Pan the, natives claim, and now renamed to honor an even more detestable false god, Caesar. Why here? Why now? Why did he ask you at this place and this time? Why did he ask at all?

"Who do people say the Son of Man is?"

As if he hadn't heard—and it can be more than a little off-putting to feel as if he already knows the answer to every question he asks.

"But what about all of you? Who do you say I am?"

Why does a five second silence feel like an hour? And you, Simon, why does every silence feel like a vacuum that you are personally obliged to fill?

"You are the Messiah, the Son of the Living God!"

As you hurled your words into that void, how wonderfully strange you felt. How can someone say a thing that he knows is true—as if he has always known it to be true—and yet be astonished at first hearing himself say it? How can you own a statement so thoroughly and yet know somehow that it isn't yours at all? And, how long did it take you before you could suck in that next breath?

Then didn't he call you blessed—the recipient of no mere human opinion but of divine revelation? Didn't he call you "Peter," the very personification of confessed faith, the rock on which he would build his church? No, you didn't begin to understand what that all meant but it wasn't that long ago. You do remember.

So how can the blessed one now be Satan? How can the foundation rock so soon become the stumbling stone? How can he say that you were speaking the very mind of God and then reverse himself and accuse you of having in mind, not the will of God, but of mortals? What did you say that was so terrible?

Jesus was going on about suffering—suffering at the hand of Israel's leaders, the very group that he as Messiah should soon be heading up. What kind of talk was this from the Man that you had just proclaimed Divine King?

"...and be killed..."

Jesus wasn't through talking but when you heard these words you were through listening. You were grabbing for his shoulder and the protest in your gut had already been launched when his words hit the air, "…and on the third day be raised." His prophecy collided with your protest: "Never, Lord! Not You! Absolutely not!"

There could be no doubt of your fidelity, could there? But that's when he said it. "Get out of my way, Satan!"

Satan!

Wait though. Is that passionate tone in his voice really anger or is it pained concern? Antagonism or resolve? And why do you feel as if Jesus is speaking less to you than someone else through you? Why suddenly are you remembering Jesus' description of his temptation in the desert? One more time you lecture yourself about thinking before opening your mouth. And you are determined to listen carefully—without interruption—to what Jesus says next…

CHAPTER 1: "...WHO LOSE THEIR LIFE FOR MY SAKE..."

Then Jesus told his disciples, "If any want to come after me, let them deny themselves, take up their cross and follow me. For any who want to save their life will lose it, and any who lose their life for my sake will find it.

Matthew 16:24, 25[1]

The question was simple enough. It should be easy and fun to answer: "Do you have a favorite saying? Is there a statement you make so often that people have come to associate its wording especially with you? Is there one quotation, original or borrowed, for which you would want to be remembered?"

Well, there's, "Just because you're miserable doesn't mean you can't have a good time." I say it often but is it really the one for which I want to be remembered? I could go at this more objectively and ask my co-workers what my signature sentence would be. I'll be right back.

An interesting experience—and all I'm going to tell you about it is that they all had far too much fun with the question. So I took it to my family. Recalling years of responding to instruction with, "I don't want to," my kids were able to reproduce even the inflection of my uniform comeback: "Then aren't you glad to know that wanting to is not one of the requirements?" They never seemed fully to appreciate such liberation—or my wisdom.

---

1   Unless otherwise noted, Scriptures are the author's own renderings and/or brief passages that the standard versions translate with virtually identical wording.

Maybe the statement is, "You have options." I remind people of that fact a lot—and this little exercise is proving that I generate options far better than I reach conclusions.

I hope this little exercise proves easier for you than it has been for me. But what if we were to ask the same questions of Jesus? Is it possible that Matthew, Mark, Luke or John leaves us with what may be the signature statement of Jesus?

You recall that Matthew, Mark and Luke are called the Synoptic Gospels because they are so similar in content. Knowing this, however, we might tend to overestimate the number of Jesus' statements that can be found in all three accounts. Far fewer are his statements found in all four accounts, the Synoptics as well as John. And we find even fewer that appear more than once in any one of the Gospels.

Yet, when we come to the Scripture that began this chapter (and takes up where the Prologue left off) we find something quite remarkable: Our Lord's words on self-denial, on gaining life through losing it, are presented with amazing consistency in all four Gospels. Mark and John record essentially the same words once each, Matthew twice, and Luke no less than three times![2]

Have we found a signature statement?

Could this process Jesus calls "self-denial" be a dominant and basic theme of his message? In fact, is Jesus really telling us that self-denial is the very essence of Christian discipleship?

At first hearing, even framed as a question, does this sound like a gross overstatement? It doesn't ring quite right, does it? Ours is the age of self-validation, self-actualization, and all other kinds of positive self-hyphenations. This talk of self-*denial*—especially as the essence of discipleship—sounds radically unpleasant, if not downright pathological. We need to know exactly what we are talking about before we embrace or reject this proposition, so hang in there with me.

There is a caricature of self-denial that sees it as little more than keeping an arbitrary list of stern restrictions meant only to drain the color and fun from life. That may be about as deep an appreciation of self-denial—or of Christianity—as some people seem to have. It's only natural to think of

---

2   Matthew 10:37-39; 16:24-26; Mark 8:34-37; Luke 9:23-27; 14:25-27; 17:33; John 12:25.

self-denial in terms of denying things or activities or pleasures to oneself. Doing without, especially for some noble or holy cause, is the meaning almost universally assigned to self-denial. If that definition is correct, our obligation to deny ourselves is filled by occasional abstinence from this or that for our religion's sake.

I grew up with a fellow who gave up watermelon and swimming for Lent every year. Of course, back then, neither of those indulgences was at all likely on the cold March plains of northern Oklahoma. Even given the common definition of self-denial, I'm afraid my friend was sorely lacking. But I'm not so sure that I have any truer grasp of Jesus' call to self-denial simply because I give up more pleasures (even available ones) more of the time. This may exhibit greater individual self-discipline without necessarily reflecting increased Biblical self-denial.

When Jesus tells me to deny self, he means just that: deny the self. Renounce, repudiate, say no to, disavow the existence of *self!* When Jesus talks of self-denial, he is calling for nothing less than the end of self, the autonomous ego, as the life principle and power.

He reveals explicitly what is involved when he continues the command to deny self with, "Take up your cross." To understand what he means I must see beyond my notions of the cross as a piece of art, a religious icon, or even a vague term that means, "personal burdens." The cross Christ calls me to bear is not an annoying family member, a financial setback, my Parkinson's Disease or any other such thing. This cross is an instrument of execution.

I must put myself in the place of the disciples who first heard this command from Jesus. At that moment they may have been expecting him to say any one of a number of things—except what they heard. I begin to sense their shock as the words, "Take up your cross" started sinking in. That command could bring to their memories only the most horrible image: a scourged criminal struggling under the weight of a plank to which he would be nailed and left to a slow and agonizing death. Bonhoeffer said it well, "When Jesus calls a man, He bids him come and die."[3]

Then there is the last third of the triune command of Matthew 16:24, "Follow me." No statement of Christian self-denial is complete—or even

---

3   Dietrich Bonhoeffer, *The Cost of Discipleship,* New York: The Macmillan Company, 1963, p. 7.

meaningful—without the concluding statement of Christ-acknowledgment. The command, then, is for nothing less than *dying* to self and *living* to Christ. Self-denial and Christ-realization are more than separate and exclusive halves. On the other hand, it may not be precisely accurate to say that they are just the same thing stated two ways. Perhaps we can think of them as the upbeat and downbeat of our song, the lub and the dub of discipleship's pulse. To think of them apart may be to think of them incorrectly. Death becomes Good News only when there is resurrection. The end of present self becomes blessing only with the recovery of the true self that God intends. That sunset is this sunrise. Dusk there is dawn here.

In each of the seven occurrences of the self-denial/Christ-realization command, the topic is the cost of following Jesus. Explicit or implicit in each passage is that life-through-death paradox that the Twelve struggled with so much. Still at the very crux of Jesus' messiahship and, thus, our discipleship, is that principal of finding life only by giving it up.

I say "crux" because it is Latin for cross, the root of our word, "crucial." When we want to talk of something of utmost importance, something that lies at the very center, we frequently—perhaps unintentionally—refer to the cross. In the same way, the Cross of Christ—his voluntary, undeserved death, which then became the source of unimaginably rich life—lies at the center of the Christian's existence.

As retold in the Prologue, Matthew 16 (and its parallels in Mark 8 and Luke 9) reveals that just before Jesus spoke of self-denial, Peter made the good confession, "You are the Christ, the Son of the living God." One important New Testament usage of the term "denial" is as the opposite of "confession" (where the latter means acknowledgment of a person rather than admission of a sin). Denial, then, is the refusal or failure to acknowledge a person. The use of these terms as opposites can be seen most clearly in passages such as Matthew 10:32, 33:

> *Therefore, whoever confesses [acknowledges, owns] me before people, I will confess [acknowledge, own] before my Father in heaven. And whoever denies [renounces, disowns] me before men, I will deny [renounce, disown] before my Father in heaven.*

Almost immediately after Peter declares that his Master is the Christ, the Lord begins insisting that such confession has powerful ramifications. At the heart of those consequences is the *denial* that must always be part of the *confession*. To own Christ is to disown self.

If I must say "no" to self it is because I must say "yes" to Christ, and nothing must prevent or dilute the totality of that "yes." The "no" heralds and enables the "yes." The "yes" enfolds and empowers the "no." The abdication coincides with the coronation. The (sinner) king is dead; long live the (sinless) King! Again, Bonhoeffer says it with simple eloquence: "To deny oneself is to be aware only of Christ and no more of self, to see only Him who goes before and no more the road which is too hard for us."[4]

"The road too hard…" How long did I try to tell myself the road wasn't too difficult, too steep for me? Then once I admitted the truth, how much longer did I keep I keep my gaze only downward despairing of all the impassible ruts and rubbish and roadblocks?

If I were in Peter's sandals and had just proclaimed, "You are the Christ!" I certainly wouldn't have expected Jesus' reply about betrayal and death. And then right there Jesus goes on to say, "Coming after me means first the end of you, an execution. Then you can follow me."

Poor Peter may not have had anything to say at *that* point. How could he? Without fuller understanding, how could all this sound like anything but madness? But Paul had years to consider the matter before he told the Philippians, "To me, living is Christ and dying is gain."[5] And it was to the Galatians that Paul gave the definitive response to the command to deny the self, take up the cross, and follow the Christ. In the midst of an impassioned dissertation on justification by grace apart from works, Paul burst forth with the profoundly wonderful assertion,

> *With Christ I have been co-crucified and I live no more; rather Christ lives in me. And what physical life I do live now, I live in faith of the Son of God who loved me and so gave himself up for my sake.*[6]

---

4   Ibid. p. 97.
5   Philippians 1:21.
6   Galatians 2:20.

Here it is again in the more familiar wording of the Revised Standard Version:

> *I have been crucified with Christ; it is no longer I who live, but Christ who lives in me; and the life I now live in the flesh I live by faith in the Son of God, who loved me and gave himself for me.*

Point for point, Paul says here precisely what Jesus says in Matthew 16:24. Jesus speaks as Master while Paul writes as disciple. One statement, first as command, then as response. Can't you hear the dialogue of these two verses?

Christ: *Paul, if you would come after me you must deny yourself.*

Paul: *Lord, it is no longer I who live at all; self is gone!*

Christ: *You must take up your cross.*

Paul: *Lord, I am crucified right along with you!*

Christ: *And you must follow me.*

Paul: *Lord, the only life I live now is your life, the faith life!*

This is a central Pauline theme. To the Philippians he insists that all the gains and accomplishments of self are only garbage to be thrown out in order to know Christ and receive the true righteousness of faith rather than the false righteousness of self.[7]

That isn't to say that there is no behavior involved in self-denial. In fact, in Colossians 3:1-4 Paul lists a number of behavioral results of self-denial. Of course, self-denial is only the upbeat, the necessary anticipation of the downbeat. Before each life-giving contraction of the heart there must be a dilation. Death to self, Paul reveals, means resurrection to Christ. It follows that the resulting new life is one set on things above rather than things of earth. But what does that mean? How does it taste?

Turning from mundane to the grander heavenly things is not self-denial, per se. It is a consequence of self-denial/Christ-realization. The disciple who has denied self surely will make new choices, will refuse certain activities, and will deny certain appetites. How can one not deny these things to self if self is gone?

Oh, I fit right in with those folks in the previous chapter of Colossians, trying to go about the Christlife backwards. Maybe I can use a method

---

7   Philippians 3:7-11.

like the one Ben Franklin describes in his autobiography: First, I'll make a list of vices I want to abandon. I'll start denying the easy ones first then the tougher ones, building up slowly to old *self*. And maybe if I'm lucky I won't ever have to get that far. Does that sound at all familiar?

The problem is that constant frustration and confusion. Which things must I deny to self? Which ones can self keep? May I indulge in this small bit of self-seeking or that harmless whiff of self-centeredness without *really* sinning? The answers never seem very certain, do they?

But what if self-denial really did start at a completely different point? What if I could begin by saying, "Indulge self, how can I? Self no longer is!" No, I doubt that the temptation will simply go away as if these words were magic. Nor will the answer to every question become crystal clear. But won't I have faced the temptation or asked the question from the truer perspective? Won't I then be able to rely, not on inadequate self to muster the strength or to find the answer, but on a fully sufficient Christ? Christ will once again take on flesh and blood, albeit imperfect flesh and blood. My lips will speak his words, my hands will perform his ministry, my legs will take him where he would go. I can even go beyond the question, "What would Jesus do?" As I yield to his Spirit, I can ask—I can truly *wonder*, "What is Jesus doing?"

The problem is that I'm not all that prepared to "throw out the garbage" as Paul did. One look at my office will tell you that I am a pack rat. And one look into my heart will tell you that I'm a hoarder there, too. It's not just a pet vice I want to withhold, or even a tasty old grudge. Perhaps even worse, I want to cling to my righteousness. I've worked hard for it.

Oh yes, Lord, I (sometimes) gladly surrender those areas of my life of which I already have made a shambles. But it seems to me that I've done such a fine job with this particular virtue. Or how about that unusual gift? Did I say "gift," Lord? Very well, it was your gift to me but haven't I developed and refined it nicely? And don't forget my *rights*, Lord—indeed, my rights and my freedoms *as* a Christian!

You say, Lord, that in you I am free? But then you say that this freedom is, at its very core, freedom from self? Surely, you aren't telling me to relinquish all the prerogatives, competencies and traits that are uniquely mine. You keep insisting that I will find myself only when I lose myself, but what does that mean? How can that possibly be the one true means of discovering all that really *is* uniquely mine? That runs counter to all logic, all instinct.

Yes, I do want out of this miry rut, this chip-on-the-shoulder, are-my-rights-being-violated foolishness. Yes, this joy-sapping, witness-warping do-it-myself religiosity does turn blessing to curse and faith to farce. But finding by losing? That is simply too confusing, too frightening, too much for *me*.

So you have to do it, Lord. You have to show me how surrender is victory, how submission is bliss, how being emptied is being fulfilled. Show me this righteousness that they say comes "only from God by atonement, not from self by attainment."

It begins by going back again to my brother Peter. And I recall that opposition of the terms "deny" and "confess" in the New Testament, particularly in reference to *disowning* or *acknowledging* persons. With that in mind, I turn to another of that handful of stories recorded in all four Gospel accounts. If Mark could skip the birth of Jesus or John could omit the Last Supper, why in heaven's name would all four evangelists preserve this story? If the early church had had a public relations director or a spin-doctor, this story might never have seen print—this story of Peter's *denial*.[8]

The apostle named Rock was solid, certain, determined. "Though everyone else may stumble, I never will," he insisted. "Even if I have to die with you, there's no way I will ever *deny* you!"[9]

There's the word! And just a few hours (and only 35 verses) later there's the deed: "I don't know what you're talking about. *I do not know the man!*"[10]

How painful was it for Peter to have this episode told and retold? Couldn't these accounts have damaged the reputation and credibility of a central figure in the early church? Tradition has it that for the rest of his life, wherever he went, Peter had to endure scornful imitations of a cock crowing, the signal of his denial.

Maybe the account is given so that we can better identify with the fallible humanity of the great apostle. Perhaps more importantly, the story

---

8   Matthew 26:69-75; Mark 14:66-72; Luke 22:54-62; John 18:25-27.
9   Matthew 26:33-35.
10   Matthew 26:70-75.

is there to remind us that any disciple, even a rock-solid Peter, can fail when relying on the strength and goodness of self.

Could it go farther even than that? After all, the story doesn't end with the denial. In the Gospels we see a weak and vacillating Peter, as much a prisoner of his own weaknesses—and strengths—as you and I. But in the book of Acts we see Peter, the Messiah's bold ambassador who actually rejoices when he is allowed to suffer for the Name of Jesus![11]

What are we to conclude? Simon, a frail, proud, selfish human being just like you and me, did become Peter, a living stone—a building block of the Kingdom.[12] But how? Only as he learned to say of *himself*, "I do not know the man," and say of Christ, "I will know only him!" Peter's story is the story of self-denial/Christ-realization. And when we embrace it as the story of our lives, then our story is, indeed, Good News!

Objection! I do just fine on my own—sometimes. Or not. But self-denial stuff is no easy matter. If Peter had such a struggle with it, how can I expect to succeed? In fact, didn't even Peter have relapses, his old self attempting its own resurrection of insurrection?[13] The Luke 9:23 account of the self-denial command may speak especially to this problem: "If any want to come after me, let them deny themselves, take up their cross daily, and follow me."

The new word jumps off the page: *Daily!* Taking up the cross of self-denial/Christ-realization is no one-time experience, is it? It's a process. But having said that, now I'm faced with an absolutely terrifying prospect. Death is a painful and frightening ordeal; are we really saying that I must undergo such agony every day? After all—and I'm quite serious when I say this—isn't one crucifixion enough? What kind of God would have me undergo such torture daily?

The answer must lie in the second part of the self-denial/Christ-realization imperative. Christ-realization is not an accomplishment; it is an acknowledgment. Or if it is an accomplishment, it is the accomplishment of Christ at work in me day by day. I don't do it. I accept it, appreciate it and embrace it. As Phillips renders it in his paraphrase of Romans 3:27, "the whole matter is now on a different plane—believing instead

---

11 Acts 5:41.
12 I Peter 2:4-5.
13 Galatians 2:11-21.

of achieving." And so I discover that this death, rather than a traumatic torture, is a sweet surrender, a letting go of our struggle.

I think a big part of what we're talking about is simple humility. By *simple* humility, I do not mean a synthetic humble-pie act that amounts to little more than lying: saying I'm not all that great when I'm fully convinced that I am even greater. Nor do I mean the crippling self-deprecation that actually believes this unique child of God, created in his image, is worthless pond scum—which amounts to little more than calling God the liar!

What I am thinking about now are those few beautiful people who seem to be quite naturally self-forgetful and sincerely interested in others. Somehow, they seem to have a center of reference other than self. Yet, where there is something wonderful about or in or through them, they neither deny it nor gloat over it. They *simply, humbly* celebrate it as God's gift.

Do you feel us getting closer now to the secret of true self-denial? Can it be so profoundly simple? As long as I am concentrating merely on denying self, I have not succeeded because self is, necessarily, ever before me. It's like trying to forget about purple elephants by constantly telling myself, "Don't think about purple elephants." *I* make *myself* painfully aware of *me* by constantly going about asking *me* how *I* should deny *self* in each given instance.

I can think of only one way to overcome such ridiculous, crippling self-consciousness. Let me illustrate with a slightly embarrassing confession. I can get so caught up in a television drama that, quite outside my own awareness, I began to mirror the facial expressions of the performers. On occasion it has been gleefully reported to me that I was even moving my lips along with the character. Then there was the time I started talking back to the TV, but that's another story...

Remarkably, I wasn't the least bit embarrassed by my performance *until* it was pointed out to me! While the slightest degree of self-consciousness certainly would have prevented such behavior, at those moments *I* was the last thing on my mind. I didn't care how silly I looked because I didn't know how silly I looked. For just those moments I cared only about the characters on the screen.

What would happen if I became that absorbed in Christ? When I am fully immersed in Christ, self-denial isn't the painful, consuming center of focus; rather it is a simple, even unavoidable reality!) Galatians 2:20 could almost be paraphrased, "Me? Me who? This is totally about Christ!"

Self-denial/Christ-realization, then, is all one thing. That's why I keep taking the time to type out those four words, two hyphens and a slash. They really constitute one term. But the area of *concentration* must be on the second half of our "word," on the downbeat of our song, on resurrection! We could almost as easily and rightly refer to self-denial/Christ-realization as self-forgetting/Christ-absorption. And it is the absorption, the realization, the acknowledgment that will fill us, consume us, redeem us!

Finally, family, whatever is true, whatever noble, whatever just, whatever pure, whatever winsome, whatever is admirable things there are—if there is any excellence, if any praiseworthiness, actively take these things into account.

Philippians 4:8

And there is Someone who qualifies on every point in Paul's list above. That Someone offers himself as the Center of all my thoughts, words and actions. He died a horrible death in order to make that offer good. Yes, praise God, one crucifixion is enough! The cross I am called to take up is the one cross of Jesus. So I can deny self only to the degree that I acknowledge Christ. He becomes my only Reality—whether self likes it or not! Even if old self seems to be quite healthy and kicking every time I look, I *deny* self—I quit looking! I go on under the assumption that self is dead, co-crucified.[14] Then I look to Christ alone to make that assumption the truth.(I look to Christ alone to make my new life real.) For the disciple, self-denial/Christ-realization is not a part of life; it is life itself. Authentic, abundant, eternal life!

---

14   The word in Galatians 2:20 is not merely *estauromai* (have been crucified); the prefix *syn* (co-, along with) has been added *(synestauromai)*.

CHAPTER 2: "...THE SCANDAL OF THE CROSS..."

As for me, may I never boast except in the cross of our Lord Jesus Christ, through whom the world has been crucified to me, and I to the world.

Galatians 6:14

Can you see it? Everyone is dressed so nicely: suits and ties, high heels and pearls. One woman looks especially graceful in her classic black dress accented with delicate jewelry; absolutely elegant in a wonderfully understated way. Her necklace features a tasteful platinum chain highlighted by one small pendant. The charm is of a very simple, highly polished design. Though smooth and stylized, the charm is an unmistakable representation of an electric chair.

I wonder if the historians could tell us when the cross started to become pretty. I don't mean beautiful. To the Christian the cross will always be beautiful. But pretty? Even apart from the physical reality of rough-hewn timbers, hammer-gouged and bloodstained, there is the transcendent reality of the cross: what *really* happened there; the unspeakable horror; the unfathomable sacrifice.

I wonder, too, what all the prettiness does to my ability to be touched by the cross, to contemplate its significance, to shed a single tear in recognition of the inescapable fact that Jesus suffered and died there for me!

Oh yes, the cross is a scene of universal magnetism. The songs and sermons, the books and essays, the sculptures and paintings, the plays and pageants and pilgrimages—doesn't the endless procession of artistic

1 Cor. 1 18, 23, 24

homage insist that we have indeed considered the cross? Touched by it? We are inundated with it!

But isn't that the problem? Couldn't there be a kind of over-exposure that blunts the meaning of the cross? To be brutally honest, don't we have to admit that the cross is a cliché?

Writers for a new sitcom want to portray a smarmy, religious buffoon. So they hang a big, gaudy cross from the actor's neck. The critics give the show negative reviews and the producer whines, "They crucified us! Call the Red Cross!" Fingering a Swiss Army knife, the director moans, "Oh great, one more cross to bear—as if these childish actors weren't enough!" Sarcastically he intones, "Forgive them, they know not what they do." And so, with gold chains, crosses, anhks and a half dozen other contradictory trinkets jangling on his chest, he jumps in his sports car and heads for the airport. On the way, he passes hospitals, insurance offices, schools and consulates that all, like his pocketknife, employ crosses in their logo (no one seems to remember why). At the airport, he boards the private jet that will whisk him to his desert get away near Las Cruces, New Mexico. The cross is a cliché.

Wait, though. Which cross do we see? A cross that is somehow romantic though perhaps a bit trite? A fantasized, plastic crucifix? Is that the cross of Christ or is it an adornment in the man-made sanctuary where we seek refuge from the real cross?

Sitting in padded pews, is our view of a hurting world a little too obscured and colorized by the stained glass through which we peer? Protected by stone walls and flying buttresses, do we take a little too much comfort in a polished and stylized cross? And as we remember the blood that was shed on the cross, does pasteurized grape juice in sterile thimbles go down just a little too easily?

The authentic cross shockingly proclaims the very thing I don't want to hear. So I turn from the cross. Or if I must come to it, I'll bring cleaning solutions, sand paper and paint.

Lord, I love you. Let me smooth the splintery edges; let me make your cross somehow less brutal, less repulsive, less real. I don't want to know that the cross is a bloody mess, a shameful scandal that must shock me and hurt me.

After all, Lord, we're all fairly good, decent folk here. We don't need or deserve to be exposed to such horror. We needn't talk of atrocity or scandal. We cannot forget our propriety. We must not be cut too deeply.

A literal cross is a scene of failure, disgrace and torture. The shame of the cross is the very antithesis of Divine Majesty. It is the ultimate affront to human dignity. Surely the only proper response is to turn away in sickened disbelief. Wasn't that what Jesus' own apostles did? Tell me again what Jesus said about love. Let me recall his blessing of the children. Just don't show me an uncensored Cross.

But without the cross there is no love and there can be no blessing.

Knowing that then, can I go beyond repulsion and denial to the compelling reality of a Savior's perfect sacrifice? I guess Jesus doesn't really need me to dignify his cross. Any such effort is doomed to result only in a pathetic sort of sacrilege. Still, the urge remains because a literal cross seems too much to bear.

The tendency has always been with us. Even before that black day, proud and weak humanity had already begun denying the reality of the cross. From the time of Peter's confession of Christ right up to the very end, Jesus repeatedly explained that he would suffer and be killed and then be raised three days later. Remember from Matthew 16:22, how Peter reacted the first time Jesus mentioned the subject? "No way, Lord! Never! Not you!" Still, there it is in the very next verse, the Lord's stern response:

> *"Get out of my way,*[15]* Satan! You're being a stumbling block to me because you are thinking not in God's but in human ways."*

And thus it has been for nearly two millennia. To us the cross is the scandal, the stumbling block, the offense.[16] But Christ insists that the real scandal or offense is this human reaction to the cross. To truly acknowledge all the cross is and says, sinful humanity must get past the basic urge to deny or alter the reality. Our problem is not only one of ignorance and indifference, though these are considerable in our time. The problem is also that sort of propriety that seeks somehow to refine

---

15   Literally, *go behind me,* an idiom very close in impact to the modern idiom, "get out of my face!"

16   The word, *skandalon,* most commonly has been rendered by these three English terms. It occurs also in Galatians 5:11 from which the title of this chapter is taken.

and sterilize the cross. After all, *our* God couldn't be responsible for such monstrous brutality, could he?

One of the earliest heresies in the church had as a main tenet the denial of a literal cross. These heretics believed that only spirit was good and that matter was evil. For God literally to become flesh, then, would be an impossible contradiction of his very essence. So they reasoned that Jesus was something or someone other than God Incarnate.

One group said that Christ only seemed to be human; his corporeality, his fleshliness, was only simulated. You might say he was God's avatar, his virtual reality. He was pure Spirit, incapable of suffering. On the cross he merely went through the motions, the formality of the Passion.[17]

Another group did not deny the fact that Jesus was flesh and blood; they simply denied that he was God. They taught that the Spirit of God entered Jesus at his baptism in so unique a measure as to effect the closest thing possible to a human personification of the Divine. But they insisted the Spirit had to leave Jesus just prior to his Passion because God, being perfect, could not suffer. So the suffering on the cross was real but it was merely human suffering.[18]

By the time John wrote the fourth account of the Gospel, these heresies were becoming widespread. So John left no room for doubt in his identification of Jesus. In the prologue he called Christ *God,* and later in that first chapter said that it was this God, this divine Word that became flesh.[19] When John came to the crucifixion he recorded a statement of Jesus that none of the other three evangelists had reported. It is the shortest of the seven recorded statements from the cross, only one word in the Greek. We might at first even question its relative significance in comparison with other utterances from the cross. But we have only to recall those false teachings that were threatening the church. Then we can understand clearly why John recalled that simple utterance, "I thirst."[20]

---

17 The Docetists began to assert influence in the first century. By the early second century their system was developed enough to receive specific refutation by Ignatius and others.

18 The Gnostic movement also began in the latter half of the first century. It gained strength in the mid-second century under the leadership of Valentinus, Marcus and others. While some Gnostics embraced a Docetic Christology, most others explained in Incarnation as summarized in this paragraph.

19 John 1:1-5; 14.

20 John 19:28.

In a thousand different ways, some subtle, some almost innocent, the heresies are still with us. With intentions that seem only the noblest we continue to avoid or explain away the God who suffers on a cross. No less divine than his Father, no less human than his executioners, lifted up toward one world while still cruelly nailed to this one, the Christ experienced a tormenting thirst that defies description. The conclusion is even farther beyond our comprehension: God chooses to suffer with and for sinful humanity! To reject this truth for some mistaken notion of protecting God's glory is to defend a most terrible glory, one capable only of damning us. The German theologian, Edmund Schlink, dramatically defines what is at stake.

> *So long as we still imagine that we must praise God's majesty and protect it against lowliness, we have not yet passionately sought God. So long as we rave about his omnipotence and holiness in contrast to the weakness and disgrace of the cross, we have not yet been confronted by God's majesty and have not yet learned to know ourselves.*
>
> *The Son of divine majesty, the Christ of supernatural fullness and power, has become so lowly that He lets men give Him a drink, so weak and helpless that nothing seems so fitting as ridicule and derision. Behold this disgrace! God's terrifying greatness has vanished in the crucified One. God is here in the midst of us—the Most Lowly and the Most Humble.*
>
> *Nothing is greater in this scene than that here God ceases to insist on His greatness and descends to become lowliest among us... Were it not for this, we must all perish. We cannot live under the wrath of the overwhelming God. Whoever thinks he can, has not yet been confronted by God's greatness. We can only deny God or curse ourselves. But we cannot establish communion with God.[21]*

But what we cannot do, God graciously does for us. It is he who spans the gulf. It is he who establishes the communion, revealing entirely new dimensions of glory and righteousness. Here is holiness so opposed to sin

---

21 Edmund Schlink, *The Victor Speaks*, Paul F. Koeneke, trans., St. Louis, Missouri: Concordia Publishing House, 1958, pp. 25, 27, 28.

that it goes beyond condemning the sinner to transcending itself, paying the price, and thus obliterating the sin.

Here is majesty so great that it surpasses all human definitions. We measure majesty in terms of size, power and aloofness. But God shows to his universe the ultimate majesty by leaving heaven to die on a cross, so that those created in his image might know the joy, above the terror, of his greatness.

Here is omnipotence immeasurably greater than power that can only crush the weak and imperfect. Here is infinite strength that allows the weak and imperfect to crush it. The flick of a finger could justly annihilate them all. Instead, that finger jerks with painful nail-driven spasms. The mighty Lion of Judah[22] could rightly devour these pathetic creatures. Instead, he closes his just and terrible jaws and lowers his head in submission to petty assault. He let mortals kill him in order that he might save them. This omnipotence is nothing less than omnipotent *love!*

How can we take all this in, this outrageous love? In the cross, God's glory has, after all, achieved its own absolute vindication in a way no mortal mind could have conceived.

But what of human dignity? Can it, too, be vindicated in the cross or must it only be crushed? We come to realize that there can be no dignity that emanates from humans in and of themselves. We cannot come to the cross with our own embellishments. We cannot strike a bargain with the One who hangs there. We cannot turn away and ask God for his Plan B. We dare not think for a moment that there could have been any other way to establish this communion with our Creator. We are mute before the cross.

We understand that this is far more than a cruel death. The point of the cross is not its physical torture, nor its ultimate crime against Innocence, nor the inhumanity of its perpetrators. Others died on crosses. Others have suffered unspeakable torment. The innocent die daily. Moment by moment humans exhibit expert and horrifying inhumanity. But the cross of Christ is unique in all of time and space. This death was chosen, willed by the

---

22 Revelation 5:5. In his *Chronicles of Narnia,* C. S. Lewis gave us perhaps the most memorable use of this metaphor for Christ: the mighty lion, Aslan. See especially his first volume, *The Lion, the Witch and the Wardrobe* (New York: Scholastic Inc., 1950), 149-152.

One who suffered it. And he died neither as another martyr nor even the greatest Martyr, but as the one—the only—Substitute.

You recall that the cross rightly belonged to a brigand, a terrorist named Barabbas.[23] The plaque that was affixed atop the Cross should have borne his name, should have listed his crimes. Instead it read, "Jesus... King."[24] Was his rightful title his only crime? Perhaps for the Romans whose high king was Caesar. But there is a higher Ruler than Caesar, and there was a weightier law that required this death.

As that Ruler of the universe gazed down upon the plaque, the name Barabbas *was* inscribed and so were his crimes. For I am Barabbas. Take out your wallet. Look at your i.d.: You are Barabbas. We may protest our dignity, our innocence or our worthiness from now to eternity but it will not change the fact that this cross is rightly ours. He died for our sins, in our place, on our behalf.

We know that, don't we? We deny our guilt, rationalize it, paint over it, coat upon coat. But we know. At some level we know that we a have a guilt that demands a Savior.

By the first century AD, crucifixion had developed to a science of exquisitely prolonged torture and death. This form of execution was all too familiar to the first readers of the Gospel. There was no need to go into detail. That may not be true today, so descriptions of crucifixion's medical horrors may serve a purpose. The scourging, the nails, the continual cramping of the muscles, the inability to take a breath, the spittle of his tormentors, the insects burrowing into his wounds; Jesus felt every one of these. But scripture does not focus on these torments at all. Rather, it calls us to consider what must have been the most excruciating pain of all. The burden of my sins and yours, our guilt and shame that he bore; what words can depict *that* agony? How dare we compare that cosmic throe with any physical pang? What calculus, what comparison would we use?

His radical, affronting grace cries out from the cross, *"In your place!"* With three simple words, he invites me to put aside my own ill-defined and pretentious dignity. *In your place*! With three simple words, he identifies with me and bids me come lose my identity in his. Lose it to find it: true identity and the only authentic dignity.

---

23   Matthew 27:15-26.
24   Matthew 27:37.

"In your place, I cried, 'Forsaken!' Now in my place, you may cry, 'Father!' I took your sinfulness; now take my righteousness. I paid your penalty; now receive my reward. I died your death for sin; now come live my life of glory. What was yours, I have taken as mine. Now what is mine, come take as yours!"

And then he cries out, "It is finished!" But there is no tone of defeat, no sigh of resignation. This is nothing less than the victory cry of a mission accomplished: "It's done. I won!" How can such words echo from a cross? They can because they are true. All really is finished on the cross. From that point on, nothing is the same. As he cries, "It is finished," he is saying as well, "Now it begins!"

Finished is the stony weight of Law's unmet demands. Begun is a law of liberty written on the heart. Finished is the darkness of ignorance; begun is the light of Christ. Finished is existence in the death that is sin; begun is the celebration that is life in the Spirit. Finished is the deformation from our fallenness; begun is the transformation into his holiness. Finished is our isolation and terror; begun is our new day in the arms of a new Love.

There was a separation but that wall has been razed; the veil is torn, the chasm bridged. In place of alienation from God there is reconciliation. The sacrifice, being perfect, must never be repeated. Christ died once, for all; there is nothing any of us can ever do to make the gift better or the work more effective. There remains only to say *finished!* to self and *begun!* to Christ. There remains only to embrace a belief lived out in total surrender. Since his righteousness is now ours, then his Father is ours, his joy is ours, his abundance is ours, his glory is ours, and his home is ours. Even now, he is preparing a place for us there. He said so.[25]

I stand, then, confronted by the cross. Shall I turn away insisting that I have no failure or that I can somehow save myself? Shall I stay only to give a mock obedience, a pretense of righteousness fashioned of compromise and self-determination? Or will I find grace to forego my self-satisfaction, safety and comfort—even my dignity? Can I simply kneel now at the cross and let the full force of its message pierce my heart? Can I let the cross of Christ crucify me, too?

As terrifying as I find it, the cross offers me only one option: If I want to be made whole, I have to be broken. If I am to be fully healed there, I

---

25   John 14:1-3.

must be mortally wounded there. If I would live with Christ in his home, I must die with Christ on his cross.

PART TWO

The Mind
of
Christ

CHAPTER 3: "AREN'T YOU WORTH MUCH MORE..."

Christ Esteem (handwritten)

For through the grace given me I say to every one of you, don't have higher thoughts of yourselves than are warranted. Rather, let those thoughts be a rational reflection of the measure of faith God has given each of you.

Romans 12:3

He was a farmhand and, on that Sunday, a prophet. Who could have known that, in one short sentence of protest, he had given what would become a rallying cry for a movement that would sweep the church for the rest of the twentieth century and beyond? He was no deep thinker; his meaning may not have been so profound or well thought through as that of the many who would follow. Still, his words were striking.

We had sung the Isaac Watts classic, *At the Cross*. This simple though proud man had refused to sing. Later all he said was, "I ain't no worm!" Within a year or two, experts were saying more or less the same thing. Before long, hymnals were being published with the revised line, "Would He devote that sacred head for such a *one* [in place of *worm*] as I?"

So was that fellow just stubborn and prideful? Or did he realize that he was made in God's image and that Jesus counted him worth dying for? That's the problem, isn't it? When the subject is self-worth (or self-esteem or self-acceptance), far too much of what is being said and written is based on that brand of carnal pride called humanism. Still, am I a worm? Or am I not worth infinitely more than the bird that eats the worm[26] Is a low view of humanity appropriately humble or is it sacrilege?

---

26   Matthew 6:26.

As a follower of Jesus, what am to think? On the one hand, David says that humanity was created only a little lower than divinity, that God has crowned us with glory and honor.[27] On the other hand, this same David used that description, *worm*, of himself at least once.[28]

Conventional wisdom tells us that self-love is not only good but absolutely necessary if we are to function well at all. In most circles, religious or secular, this assumption is beyond debate. But when we turn to scripture for a word on self-love, the one explicit reference we find is II Timothy 3:2. There Paul talks of bad times to come in which people will be unholy, arrogant, brutal lovers of money and pleasure. And throughout the opening verses of that chapter, Paul has other strong words to describe these people but he begins the list by calling them *lovers of self.*

What are we to make of all this? Deny self or accept self? Doesn't one forbid the other? Or is it really that simple? Some of the most self-absorbed people you will ever meet are those who are filled with self-hatred. When I stop to think about it, I have to admit that the worse I feel about myself, the more I tend to dwell on myself. So much is this the case that our post-Freudian age would rather assume that the loudmouthed know-it-all is suffering more from inferiority than a case of honest conceit. More often than not, that diagnosis is correct!

There is a perverted understanding of self-denial that equates it with self-loathing. We certainly can see *that* as an opposite of self-acceptance. But at the heart of Christian self-denial is a positive self-forgetfulness, not a crippling self-contempt. Self-denial isn't self-abuse, it's self-release. Even the purely humanistic advocates of self-esteem agree that healthy self-acceptance is not obsession with self.

Part of our problem may be the fact that we are dealing with two distinct but overlapping arenas; one is psychological and the other is spiritual. No doubt, deeper thinkers would tell us that we are equating apples and oranges. But for most of us, the distinction isn't as important as that overlap.

---

27 Psalm 8:5.
28 Psalm 22:6. It might be argued that David was just ironically reflecting the view of his enemies. Bildad, in Job 25:6, says of humanity in general, that we are *worms* but the reliability of his assessment could also be questioned. In Isaiah 41, God assures Israel that, though their enemies are formidable while they are a *worm,* he will help them.

Suppose you ask, "Who am I, and how am I?" Suppose that I reply, "Are we speaking spiritually or psychologically?" You probably wouldn't find my response very helpful or reassuring. And after all, isn't it ultimately our spiritual state that grounds our psychological state? Two psychologists, one who thinks we are merely evolved slime and one who believes we are made in God's image, may agree on a number of things, but not on the most fundamental.

We must be careful not to read modern psychotherapeutic content or intent into biblical texts that are clearly speaking to other realms. But I am convinced that a broad, general biblical psychology can be delineated. I am further convinced that our theology must inform and undergird even our more specific and exhaustive psychological methodologies. So may I, for our purposes, speak of a spiritual self that grounds our psychological self?

But that still leaves us two selves that absolutely must be distinguished, the old self and the new. Starting with this distinction we will be able to arrive at the fundamental truth on this matter—let's call it the "essential paradox": Self-denial is the one path to legitimate self-acceptance.

Christ does not want his sisters and brothers crippled by a self-deprecating distortion of humility (more on this later). He wants us to experience life in abundance. We are creatures created for glory. Yet, it is God's glory and it is glory of which we all have fallen short.[29] But Christ is God's own Shekinah, his visible glorious presence; he has come to free us from whatever holds us back from the glory of God. He does this by co-crucifying our old self with him and by resurrecting a new self with him.[30] Who is this new self? It is *no longer I but Christ!*

The time has come at last. Backed into the final corner, I admit defeat. I cannot do this—any of this—this living, this being, this purpose for which I was created. I can never get it right. Tried and found guilty, I surrender to the executioner. He takes a nail in one hand, his hammer in the other, and bends over my helpless form, stretched upon the cross. Terrified, I would resist. Hopeless, I cannot. I await the first blow of the lifted hammer.

---

29 Romans 3:23.
30 Romans 6:4; II Corinthians 5:17; Ephesians 4:22-24; Colossians 3:1-17; etc.

But suddenly, between my flesh and the executioner's spike is the guiltless body of One who condescends to be my Champion, my Substitute, my Savior. And when the hammer comes down upon the nail, his is the flesh that is pierced.

But what is this? I am pierced, too! Not by cold metal but by white-hot love! And what is this body that is being pierced? It's what I have called "me" but why do I now recognize it as something less than me, something other than the person created in God's image? As the nail's point stabs deeper, I feel more and more as if it is cutting through some sort of shell, a sclerosed cocoon of callous living and crusted pride. That flesh, if now I can even call it flesh, still trembles and resists the spike. But a deeper tissue, robust with life and color, begins to welcome this liberation, this shedding of its distorted mantle. Living pores breathe as if for the first time. *I* breathe as if for the first time, expiring the old, inspiring the new. What I had thought could bring only pain has brought relief. What I thought could be only annihilation has become exhilaration. Sin is slain by grace and I am—oh yes, I am born again! *No longer I but Christ.*

Yet, this Christ, though constant and consistent, is never redundant. He doesn't shape me with a cookie cutter. What he has created anew is still someone unique in temperament, giftedness and history. He truly has recreated a *person* with a distinct personality and purpose—as distinct as Jesus was from his cousin John.[31] Peter and Paul, Matthew and Luke, extrovert and introvert, sanguine and choleric, you and me—each distinct, each a work in progress. Yet each can say in truth, *"No longer I but Christ!"*

I hope, then, that you will understand as I propose a new terminology. Rather than debating matters of "self-worth," "self-love" or "self-esteem," can you and I talk of "*Christ*-esteem"? We have to admit that the Bible simply does not say I must love or accept myself. It does tell me I absolutely must accept Jesus. It says that Jesus accepts me, even before I am acceptable, even while I still don't know how to accept myself! Praise God, the blood of Christ is all-sufficient for my salvation; I need nothing more—not even a positive self image!

If we stopped right there that would be absolutely enough. But this regeneration touches every facet of my life, even my self-image. So Christ-

---

31   Matthew 11:18, 19.

esteem begins to take hold. He, by sheer, unmerited grace, esteems me. As his blood pours out he declares, "This is what you are worth to me!" How can I respond with anything less than complete esteem for this my Lord and my God? And if it truly is no longer I but Christ, then this esteem, flowing from and back to Christ, is flowing through and saturating the new self. So call it self-esteem if you wish but know that from beginning to end it is really Christ-esteem.

He has taken this clay jar and put his treasure in it;[32] he has made it a vessel of glory, a conduit of divine love. The old self-loathing blocked the flow of love between God and me, between others and me. But as that self is denied and Christ is realized, the blockage is removed. Love flows. Down and up, in and out. Call it self-love if you wish but know that from beginning to end it is God-love.

I have heard Good News and it tells me that while I may not be *worthy* of Christ's redeeming love, he has proclaimed me *worth* it. I dare not insult that love either by maintaining that I can earn it or by insisting that I am not worth it. Rather, having accepted Christ and his love, I can now accept the uniqueness of who and what I am. I can do this, not by arbitrarily pronouncing myself and everyone else "OK," but by accepting the judgment of almighty God. If my self-acceptance—my "OK-ness"—were based on myself, I would soon cry out with Paul, "What a wretched person I am!"[33] But as Paul goes on to say, "Thanks to God...there is now no condemnation for those in Christ Jesus!"[34] No condemnation. None. Zero. God forbid that I condemn where he has said there is to be no condemnation.

I do have love within myself. Not self-satisfaction, not self-aggrandizement, and certainly not self-delusion. Rather, I have an authentic love founded in Christ, who is the Truth. It is a love of Christ's indwelling Spirit, who accepts me as I am while still calling me on to perfection. Thus Paul continues:

> *For those who live according to the flesh set their minds on*
> *things of the flesh, but those who live according to the Spirit*
> *set their minds on the things of the Spirit. To set the mind*

---

32 II Corinthians 4:7.
33 Romans 7:24.
34 Romans 7:25; 8:1.

on the flesh is death, but to set the mind on the Spirit is life
and peace. For this reason the mind that is set on the flesh
is hostile to God; it does not submit to God's law—indeed
it cannot, and those who are in the flesh cannot please God.
But you are not in the flesh; you are in the Spirit, since the
Spirit of God dwells in you.

Romans 8:5-9a (NRSV)

Christ grants me a new nature and then he calls me to act accordingly. But with the demand comes the power to respond.[35] So a wondrous cycle is introduced by which he grows me, step by step, in his likeness. He grants me a new and genuine sense of identity and worth. I am *inspired* to grateful, godly action. That behavior, in turn, increases the sense of identity and worth and the cycle continues as my mind is set on the things of the Spirit. As I let him work in me, he grows me into whom he wants me to be. As I come to realize that growth, I learn to trust him even more, which leads to greater growth—you see the process.

That mindset will be our focus in the next two chapters. We'll learn a practical way to live in this cycle of personal growth through self-denial/Christ-realization.

For now, though, there remains only one other matter. I hope by now that you and I are good enough friends that I can tell you this. This chapter and the next two will do you a great disservice if you read them merely as one more set of instructions for gaining self-esteem. They are not written so that, having read them, you will like yourself a little better. Their goal is infinitely higher than that.

I happen to know that you are a wonder, precious and special. But in this moment, turn your gaze away from yourself to an even greater Wonder. See the eternal love of the King of kings. Esteem him. Be immersed in him. Be saturated with him. Be transformed by him.

Now it just so happens that, because he created you and loves you, when you lose yourself in him you *will* find yourself. When you look deeply into his heart, you will discover yourself there. The issues of poor self-image will be resolved—dissolved in the one true solution. But this is a serendipity, icing on the cake, a sweet side effect. The thing itself is to

---

35   See Philippians 2:12-13 and Colossians 3:1-17.

let go of yourself and let Jesus take hold of you. Give up the frustrating struggle to accept yourself; instead, accept Christ.

But know that it has to be on his terms alone. He is not for hire as personal trainer, guru or shrink. He doesn't want to be your security blanket or your cheerleader. He will be your Savior and your Lord. He is not available as a *means* to any other end for he himself is the Beginning and the End, the Alpha and Omega of all life.

So what shall we do, you and I? Spend our lives trying to love our old unlovable selves? Find ever more elaborate smoke and mirror techniques by which to impress everyone, hoping that maybe this time the smoke-and-mirrors will fool us, too? More obsession, more compulsion, more works of the flesh? I've tried that and I'm so tired. What if we just abandon that pursuit? What if we just decide to know nothing but Christ and him crucified?[36] Oh, just look at him there! Doesn't he shine? Have you ever seen such brilliance, such splendor? And who is this—this radiant, new creature mirrored in the gleam of his glory?

---

36   I Corinthians 2:2.

CHAPTER 4: "...SET YOUR MIND..."

If, then, you have been co-resurrected with Christ, let your every endeavor be directed upward where Christ is seated at God's right hand. Set your minds on those upper-level, rather than earthly, things. For you died, and with Christ your life is now hidden in God.

Colossians 3:1-3

Have you ever seen the Great Pyramid of Khufu in Egypt? One of the seven manmade wonders of the world, it is an awesome testimony to the artistry, skill and determination of the ancients. For millennia, people have puzzled and argued over just how it could have been built. In this chapter you and I are going to visit an even greater pyramid. Its construction, too, has been the subject of much confusion, debate and wonder. And as masterful as the Egyptian builders were, their ability pales in comparison to that of the Master Builder who created this pyramid.

On our way I want to ask you a personal question. The last time you went to a church service or the last time you did a good deed, why did you do it? Did you just feel like it? Did you do it to please someone you didn't want to disappoint? Or did you do it simply because it was the right thing to do? We can agree that there are many reasons, even wrong reasons, for doing right things. But there is one right reason that is consistently reliable, a source of power and legitimate motivation.

Here we are now at the pyramid. It is divided into three great levels or stories. Each of these segments represents the three fundamental

Not someone who fails to do what He intends.

Hypocrite. ~~attempts to do what they never intended.~~

Someone who never intends to do what he pretends.

We all fail at times.

38

motivations of behavior.[37] We can label the bottom story, the broadest section, *FEELING*. Behavior at this level is motivated by emotions, instinctive drives, desires and fears. We are born with the ability to act on this level, so we might designate it also as the *INFANT* level.[38]

Now let's move up one section to a behavioral level that we started learning almost from birth, the basis for more and more of our behavior as we grew into childhood. Since the structure is a pyramid, this level isn't as broad as the bottom story. It isn't quite as strong or instinctive as *FEELING,* but it runs a close second. We can call this section *APPROVAL,* the *CHILD* level.

It is amazing how soon babies learn to recognize the looks and sounds of parental approval, and disapproval. Even more amazing is how long the need for that approval, and the fear of that disapproval, may stay with them. How many of us, even as adults, still carry our parent-ghosts wherever we go, seeking but never quite feeling their applause?

Before we move up to the top level, certain points about the other two merit our consideration. First, there is nothing wrong with feelings. They are God's gifts. To have no feelings is to be less than God created us to be. In fact, an emotion in and of itself is neither right nor wrong; feelings are non-moral. They are simple responses to stimuli which God's word neither condemns nor demands. They enter into the moral arena only when we allow them to become willful thoughts or actions.

To be sure, the Bible does encourage us to cultivate and nurture certain affections. We are to find our delight in the Lord.[39] And Paul tells the Romans that they are to show cheerful mercy while they abhor evil and love each other dearly.[40] Clearly, though, these are cultivated affections, not unwilled, reflexive emotions.

We can have "mere" affections and we can have "set" affections. By "set affection" I mean a combination of feelings and will, the determination to nurture certain dispositions. When we set our affections, we decide to enjoy what we need to enjoy doing and being in Christ. We may naturally

---

37 The author is grateful to Jerry Townsend and Carl Thompson of Life Awareness Associates, for inspiration behind many of the concepts and illustrations in this chapter and the next.

38 James 4:1-3 paints a vivid picture of FEELING/INFANT level behavior.

39 Psalm 37:4.

40 Romans 12:8-10.

("in the flesh," as the Bible puts it) tend to find pleasure in any number of things. But over time we can develop a more discriminating taste that does indeed delight in the things of the Lord. I'll say more about this in the next chapter.

So while there is an overlap between emotion and volition, their distinction is important because it is precisely at this point that old Satan often tricks us into accepting defeat when we don't have to. Say he besets me with some wrongful desire to which I say a firm, "No!" Does the temptation vanish immediately? That usually isn't my experience. As often as not the temptation stays right with me. James 4:7 promises that if we resist the devil, he will flee—but it doesn't reveal the timetable! So must I conclude that I have thereby sinned? I think that Satan would like me to think so but the fact is, I haven't. Temptations become sins only when I give them permission, when I say yes either to the mental fantasy or the actual deed.

Of course there are legitimate, righteous ways of permitting emotions and drives into the realm of willful thought or action. Sexual arousal, for example, can be expressed towards one's mate in appropriate ways and at appropriate times. In fact, this is one of those affections that is to be cultivated or set. Marital love is a uniquely wonderful combination of emotion and will. It is the divine amalgamation of eros and agape—of desire and deliberate good will. Eros brings hearts together, agape makes those hearts one. The eros lends passion to the agape while the agape lends constancy to the eros.

We may find ourselves subject to all kinds of urges. But we can weigh each one; we can consider which urge merits action. The urge to run through the grass barefoot is a perfectly legitimate feeling (as are other emotions in and of themselves) and it may have several occasions for appropriate fulfillment. But there may be times when the urge must remain just that.

You know the one dependable thing about feelings, don't you? Their undependability! Emotions are not subject to logic, reason or expediency. They are, in a word, erratic. Often, we can trace their cause; almost as often we can't. So we settle for that classic of articulate and precise diagnoses, *I musta got up on the wrong side of the bed!*

When I really think this matter through, not only do I want everyone else to base their actions on something other than raw emotion, I have to admit that my own life would be miserable if my feelings determined all my behavior. My generation coined the sayings, "If it feels good, do it," and "Go with your feelings." It's way past time to rethink those clichés.

But if I'm not careful, I'm likely to exchange slavery to my emotions for slavery to another's emotions: If it makes *you* feel good, I'll do it. Just tell me I'm a good boy when I do. Again, there is nothing wrong with approval. And there is much right with seeking to serve others and live at peace with them. Scripture is full of examples and applications of the Golden Rule.

The problem comes when behavior is determined solely on the basis of human approval.[41] If approval is my only motivation, I could even end up sacrificing your welfare in favor of your approval. If you've ever dealt with a willful child or an addicted adult, you know exactly what I mean.

Some of my most difficult decisions as a parent were those that had to be made even though they incurred the disapproval of my children. My kids and I not only love each other, we've almost always liked each other—a lot. But there were times I had to remind myself that my goal wasn't to be liked; that the ultimate judge of my parenting was Someone other than my children. I still can see those angry eyes glaring back at me as if I had totally betrayed them. I still can hear the echo of the bedroom door shutting me out. And I still recall how many times I turned to Janet or she to me to strengthen our resolve, to hear the other say, "No, it's not fun, it's not popular, but it's right."

As a Christian counselor, I believe that my counselees and I can be friends who not only trust each other but enjoy our times together. If the therapeutic process can be fun, so much the better! But, again, fun is not the goal. As much as it may go against my nature, I must, at every juncture, be willing to let clients get angry with me. I must be ready for them to hate me if that is the price of speaking the truth in love. I am there to facilitate their healing, not to win their vote for Counselor of the Year.

Shane was the willful child *and* the addicted adult. Darla had to admit that what she fell in love with and married was the fine figure out on the football field. What she got was a man/child who acted as if he were the

---

41 Jesus gave several strong indictments of APPROVAL/CHILD level behavior; see, for example, Matthew 6:5, 16.

only person in the universe. All other beings were ancillary to Shane. Because he and he alone loved the movie *Billy Jack,* that had to be the name of their son. Because he was a quarterback, Billy had to be a quarterback. Because his ego was insatiable, everyone else's had to be abused. He had to be superior; therefore, everyone else had to be inferior.

For years, Shane hurled one stone of insult after another at his wife and his son. And one upon another, those stones piled up into impenetrable walls. It wasn't that Darla and Billy didn't try; in fact, they lived for Shane's approval. Darla sincerely believed that it was her lifelong duty as a Christian wife to please and appease her husband, even when he was dead wrong.

Finally, when Shane's cruelty had evaporated the last drop of mutual esteem, and when his sexual addictions had doused the last spark of affection, the marriage ended. Shane attended just one more of Billy's games. The son had indeed inherited the father's athletic gift. He had made some spectacular plays that night; his game was almost flawless. But in the closing minutes, he threw one interception that nearly cost them the game. The opposing team was threatening to score the go ahead touchdown when, mercifully, the clock ran out.

As Billy headed toward the locker room, Shane ran out onto the field after him, yelling for all to hear, "What were you thinking? Where were you looking? You couldn't have *made* it any easier for that guy to catch!"

Billy turned around and said this farewell to his father: "What you mean to say is that you're really proud of me. Right, Dad?" He turned and walked away, leaving Shane where he had always been: all to himself.

Of course, the young child doesn't have a fully developed sense of right and wrong, wise and foolish. Her volitional capacity—her ability to make independent moral choices—is not yet fully developed and integrated. She must of necessity rely heavily upon parental direction and, yes, approval. But with each passing year, her parents have the task of helping her make more and more of her own decisions, choices based not on applause but on a firm sense of right.

This brings us to the top level of motivation and behavior. Now the pyramid has become quite narrow; this level is the least easy, the least natural, and the least common. This is the level of *CONSCIENC*E. By the time a person enters adolescence he should have attained a considerable degree of personal moral responsibility, the capacity to choose independently to do the right thing.[42] In religious circles they call this "the age of accountability." If we can define an adult, in terms of volition and behavior, as one who does have a fully integrated conscience, then we have arrived at the *ADULT* section of the pyramid.[43]

Conscience, of course, is much more than that "little voice" that haunts us when we do something wrong. Conscience is *that faculty through which responsible choices are reached on the basis of the realities involved.* These realities include the situational facts but they begin with the moral and ethical standards to which one is committed.

I stunt my children's consciences if I bring them up without adequate instruction and discipline of the ability to override, to defer and to properly channel their own desires. But if all I teach my children is, "Just do what you're told," I fail them just as miserably. What will they do, to whom will they listen when I am no longer there to tell them? My task is not merely to make them answerable to me and my conscience but to help them grow fully integrated consciences of their own. They then will be able to make the right decision regardless of what they are being told and regardless of who might be looking. They will recognize what is right and do it simply because it is right.

Still, even a developed conscience can be seared over. It may be abused so often that it becomes calloused. It may be so subtly, so gently and "innocently" desensitized that it becomes numb. Or it simply may be ignored so long that it atrophies. Romans 1:18-32 details this tragic decay.

But the disciple can have his conscience revitalized, resensitized and fully integrated by the gracious power of God. For the Christian, conscience has become the *CHRIST-CENTERED CONSCIENCE (C3).* This conscience is not only centered *on* Christ, it is centered—corrected, calibrated, informed—by Christ. It is a God-directed conscience, not only

---

42 But he may be approaching his mid-twenties before the part of the brain that houses that function "comes on line" completely.

43 In developing the ideas of this chapter, some of the language used sounds similar to the terminology of Berne's Transactional Analysis and Missildine's "Inner Child" paradigm. While there are similarities, some even useful, it would be best to let those schools of thought have their own definitions of shared terms, and to allow the concepts of this chapter to stand on their own with their independent definitions as well.

directed by God, his Spirit and his word but toward God, his kingdom and his glory.

The conscience is kept growing and functional not only through consistent use but through continuing surrender to the Holy Spirit and the nurturing of that relationship. In other words, there is ongoing communion with God in prayer and praise, meditation and reading of scripture, as well as fellowship in the body of Christ, his church. Without this Spirit-nurture, my conscience wears and fades just like any other ability I leave unattended. With time, it grows deaf and nearsighted. With Christ, it grows keen and strong.[44]

There is more good news about the conscience. It is conscious! Why is that so good? Well, sometimes I know how I feel, why I feel it, and how it is affecting my behavior. But often the underlying cause is subconscious, outside my awareness. How often have I pondered, "Why in the world did I do a thing like that? What was I thinking?" Even more perturbing, family members or co-workers have sometimes sensed my mood before I have. Have you ever had this conversation?

"What's wrong with you?"

"Nothing..."

"Oh yes there is! You'd better check again. What is it?"

"I'm *FINE*, OK?!"

"Whatever..."

I just love those special moments when I get to be reminded of how out-of-touch I can be with my own feelings. After all, I'm the guy who daily encourages people to honestly face their own emotions. Of course, that's my excuse: I'm far too busy attending to everyone else's feelings to pay any attention to my own.

Much the same can be said of my need for approval. Like many others of my generation, I was raised to be a lifetime member of the Royal Order of the Clean Plate. We were led to believe that eating everything on our own plate somehow helped the starving children around the world. Maybe that's why after 40+ years my favorite Dennis the Menace cartoon is still the one in which his dad said, "You know, there are children across the

---

44 I Corinthians 1:12 is an excellent summary statement of a life lived at the C3/ADULT level. Psalm 51 is a remarkably beautiful example of a return to that level.

ocean who would give anything for the food you are wasting." Dennis replied, "Name three."

So, through much of my adult life, I automatically, unwittingly cleaned my plate, even when I was full and the bathroom scales were telling me bad things. Even after gaining insight about what I do, unless I remember to give a conscious override command, I will repeat that same old needless behavior. I confess also that I have done things purposely and consciously just for the applause. Sometimes, though, I don't even realize what I'm doing or why.

But I no longer have to accept that grand lie of our post-Freudian age the lie that says I am a mere puppet of all those drives and neuroses hidden somewhere deep inside. By the power of God's indwelling Spirit, I can choose to go directly to my C3 and do what is best, what is right, rational, reasonable, realistic and righteous! I can make that choice when I feel like it and when I don't, when it gains me approval and when it doesn't. Because it is conscious, the conscience can choose to take control over the other two stories of the pyramid.[45] *The conscience says that the conscience rules.* Let me explain.

When I was a kid, there was a peculiar novelty item on the market. It was a mysterious-looking black cube about five inches square. It bore no words of instruction or any other clues about its function except a single toggle switch on top, next to what appeared to be a little trap door. When you flipped the switch, the box would begin to vibrate and make all kinds of intriguing mechanical sounds. The door would start to open slowly as a tiny, plastic hand emerged. The hand would creep toward the switch until it was a hair's breadth away. Quite suddenly, it would flip the switch off and pop back down inside as the door snapped shut. Then only stillness. For what seemed to me a lot of money, you could buy a machine that did nothing but turn itself off!

God has given us a tool that does just the opposite. Because it is conscious, the conscience can turn itself *on*. If I told you to become

---

45 Everything in this chapter and the next assumes normal brain function and chemistry. While many emotional disorders are of medical origin, it is not within the scope of this book to address those conditions. But we who presume to offer counsel will do great disservice to others if we ignore (or treat as godless pseudo-science) the medical aspects of mental health. It is just as proper and godly to correct a serotonin imbalance as it is to correct an insulin imbalance. Shame on us if we ever leave anyone doubting that fact.

deliriously happy right now, or horribly terrified, you probably couldn't do it. You could simulate those emotions. You could even initiate a series of behaviors that might eventually produce the emotions themselves. But feelings, drives and needs simply cannot be turned on and off like the little black box. But at any waking moment you and I can decide to act rationally and conscientiously. That's good news! Life's path can be chosen. In Christ, you and I are freed to step out with volitional reality and integrity. We can know Truth and we can be true. We don't have to trudge like mindless slaves through a Never-Never Land of determinism. We don't have to be the victims of our past or our passions. We can be the co-champions with Christ!

CHAPTER FIVE: "...TRANSFORMED BY RENEWAL OF THE MIND"

Now, the Lord is the Spirit, and where the Spirit of the Lord is, there is freedom. And with unveiled faces seeing the glory of the Lord in the mirror, we are being transformed into that very same image, from one degree of glory to the next, by means of the Lord the Spirit!

II Corinthians 3:17, 18

"Just use your bank card!" The insistent preschooler is already quite familiar with the phenomenon of paying with plastic, and of ATM's, the gumball machines of currency. But it will still be awhile before she has any understanding of banking accounts. You know what happens in the interim. Every time she wants to make a purchase and Mom or Dad says there's not enough money, the child responds, "So use your card." Thus begins the education on the workings of banks. Hopefully the lesson is learned before she carries her own card. Some don't seem to complete the learning experience until they've paid some overdraft and return fees.

Your knowledge of banking can help you in this chapter. Imagine a bank that deals in the currency of *acceptance* rather than dollars. When Christ through grace accepts us, he gives us a new self that we, too, can accept. That is when he opens an inexhaustible account for us in the Bank of Acceptance. As with any bank, this one has a specific way for us to transfer funds into an "account." We can make deposits and withdrawals from the checking account. And, yes, overdrafts are possible, too. So it is important to understand how this bank operates.

Let's begin by familiarizing ourselves with the currency, acceptance. What does it look like? How does it act? What is it made of?

First, it is an inward *joy*. This is something more than happiness. Happiness, as we are using the term here, refers to an elusive emotion. In English, the root, "hap" suggests uncertainty. *Hap*piness is a *hap*hazard thing that sometimes *hap*pens to *hap*pen, and sometimes, *hap*ly, doesn't *hap*pen, in which case, life may feel rather *hap*less. To make this happiness the goal of life is to discover just how elusive and fickle it is.

In contrast, joy, as we are using the term here, abides. Joy is more than emotion; it is a conscious attitude, a set affection, a fruit of the Spirit.[46] It is the bliss that abides through periods of tears as well as of laughter. It is the spirit within—and the Spirit within—that remains constant in the affirmation, "Whatever my lot, Thou hast taught me to say it is well with my soul."[47]

Accompanying this joy within myself comes the capacity once again to make *promises* to myself. Sooner or later, my old self gives up on making promises, setting personal goals, establishing covenants and commitments in the heart. "Why bother? I'll just break them again, and I don't want any more of that awful disappointment." I know I can't trust myself— good thing I don't have to. I can trust the Holy Spirit who is and makes trustworthy. When the power behind the promise is the Spirit of Christ within, there is a genuine basis for trust. I trust in his redeeming, sanctifying work in me. So now I can make promises; I can be trustworthy.

Transformation does take place one step at a time. Final perfection awaits only on the other side. So how does this acceptance work when I do slip, when I break my promise? What does the currency of acceptance do when I fail? It experiences *forgiveness*. It accepts not only the righteous standard, but also the truth of Christ who says to the repenting heart, "Neither do I condemn you,[48] nor, then, must you. Get up now and let's move on."

Acceptance grows in the fresh air of grace, within the realm where there is no condemnation; none received, none given—not even to self.

---

46   Galatians 5:22.
47   From the words of Horatio Spafford's great hymn, *It is Well with My Soul.*
48   John 8:11.

For this is the new self; the old self has already been condemned and executed.

There are other elements to this acceptance but we'll list just one more here: *love.* We've spoken of that divine flow: it pours down from God, creating an inner fountain that streams back up to its Source, even as it pours out to others. In the process, this love floods throughout the self.

What, then, has become of my alienation and isolation? I belong to Christ. I belong in his family. I belong! What has happened to my inadequacy and incompetence? "I can do all things through Christ who strengthens me!"[49] And where is the worthless worm? He is being metamorphosed into a glorious winged creature of eternal worth!

At the Bank of (Rejoicing, Promising, Forgiving, Loving) Acceptance, I can perform several different kinds of transactions. I can make a deposit, although not in the original account. The blood of Christ totally and continually fills that main account. In him alone I have full acceptance. My deposit, then, is actually a transfer into the working account of a realized and actualized *sense* of that acceptance. In other words, this is how I experience firsthand—personally and practically—what I know to be true objectively and unconditionally: God loves me and keeps me. The working account is where creed becomes deed. This is where what I know becomes what I feel and what I do. This is where faith gets real. I get to make deposits in *that* account.

I can also make withdrawals, diminishing my *sense* of who I am in Christ. Yes, as with regular bank account, withdrawals can be made and trouble results when they exceed deposits. There is decreased ability to experience the power of that joy, promise, forgiveness and love—that acceptance. Make no mistake; the power is still "on," the acceptance is still there, when I sense it and when I don't. But there are ways of increasing and decreasing our perception of it.

Both transactions take place through the medium of behavior. All responsible behaviors are deposits. All irresponsible behaviors are withdrawals. It really is as simple as that. But we must be very clear and certain of what constitutes responsible behavior. This behavior is not a response to one's own feelings, drives and emotions. To act on the basis

---

49   Philippians 4:13.

of these is not responsible; it is infantile, operating on the lowest level of our pyramid.

Nor is the deposit a response to the demands and standards of others. In and of itself, that level of responsibility is childish (second story approval level). When we speak of responsibility here, we are talking about the only legitimate adult responsibility, responsibility to God, to truth, and thus, top-level responsibility to that Christ-Centered Conscience.

"To thine own self be true." Shakespeare may have said it first but no one has said it more than we have in this age. The disciple certainly must be true to self, but what a different self it is! It is not the emotional, approval-needy, old self but only the new self controlled by the Christ-Centered Conscience. To be responsible to Christ and to the conscious centered in and by Christ is the only way to be true to self. Anyway, how could I be true to my emotions when they are so erratic? "Truth" would change almost by the minute. Or how can I be true to an approval-addicted self when gaining one person's approval so often earns another's disapproval?

I once led a discussion about some of the less romantic areas of Christian service. One member seemed to sum up the group's feelings with these words, "There's no sense in sending myself on a big guilt trip about that. My heart simply isn't in it and it would be sheer hypocrisy for me to volunteer."

An older woman who hadn't said anything up to this point finally spoke in slow and deliberate words which none of us were soon to forget. "I'm deeply troubled by what I've heard here—truly confused. I'll have to go home and think a lot of things back through if what you all say is right. You see, I just spent the night sitting up with a patient at the hospital. I didn't know her and I didn't enjoy the sleepless night. I did it because it had to be done. I really did think I was acting out of Christian love. But now I must deal with the fact that I may have been showing nothing more than hypocrisy..."

She was the one who taught the class that day.

Yes, many Christians do stretch themselves too thin confusing compulsion for faith and guilt for piety. And like the Pharisees we all do downright professional jobs of weighing down ourselves and others with buckets full of crazy "shoulds." Certainly, questions about gifts and passions and limits are all legitimate. But can't we be done once and for all with that foolish notion, "If I don't feel it, I'm a hypocrite to do it"? Hypocrisy is not the occasional violation of one's feelings. Hypocrisy is claiming to be or do that which we have no intention of being or doing. (The ultimate hypocrisy, then, is to call myself a disciple while living by the dictates of my emotions.)

I can make two types of deposits in the Bank of Acceptance. The first is the Responsible/Happy deposit. Sometimes what I want to do and what I ought to do are the same thing. Praise the Lord! In fact, wise is the person who develops the lifestyle and the relationships that enable the highest degree of congruity between all three motivational levels, Feeling, Approval, and Christ-Centered Conscience. For example, I usually enjoy taking part in the Lord's Day assembly. And the majority of my associates approve of my attendance. But the *reason* I attend is because that is God's will for me.

When "ought" and "want" are at opposite poles, I still can make a deposit, a Responsible/Unhappy deposit. Some will tell me that this is unhealthy, stifling and pointless. I admit that it may feel uncomfortable— or even downright miserable—at the moment. But I know that a solid balance of *joy* is being built during this brief sacrifice of happiness. In place of fleeting pleasure there is a deepening sense of that worth, that acceptance and worth I have in Christ. And in the long run, there simply is no comparison.

On the night Jesus was arrested, his prayer was hardly one of eager giddiness. Nevertheless, "for the joy set before him he endured the cross…[50]

I can also make two kinds of withdrawals. The first is the Irresponsible/Unhappy withdrawal. God provides his children with an alarm system that helps them recognize when a costly withdrawal is being made. The disciple with the fully integrated conscience will find consistently that violating the conscience sooner or later feels miserable.

At times, counselees want help in getting rid of guilt feelings. But first we must determine whether the feelings are based on objective, true guilt. If, in fact, they did sin, the feelings that they are experiencing are healthy and appropriate products of conscience. And it is the sin that first must be resolved. But guilt feelings are not always the direct result of actual guilt.

---

50   Hebrews 12:2.

For example, they may be the phantoms of past, forgiven offenses or they may stem from manipulation by others (an APPROVAL level problem). In such cases we are then correct to begin with the feelings themselves. Otherwise, we can, though it sounds odd, rejoice in the misery when it appropriately alerts us to those destructive withdrawals.

Finally, there is an Irresponsible/Happy withdrawal, but it is made in a different realm from the other three transactions. The first three are made in a state of reality and rational awareness. But one must cross over into a state of fantasy in order to directly violate the conscience and then feel only good about it. I am convinced that the more often we cross that border and the longer we stay, the more we risk not only our moral and spiritual integrity but our mental health as well. You often hear it said these days that our world is going crazy. What else should we expect when so many insist that the way to happiness is, in effect, the irrational suicide of conscience? What else can happen if we carelessly keep bouncing checks and living lives of plastic—over the limits?

I know of a marriage almost destroyed by a wife who wrote checks whenever she wanted, without the slightest thought about the availability of funds. Her husband had paid thousands in fees for insufficient funds before she finally sought help. I know a man—you probably do, too—who ended up behind bars because he decided that as long as he had plastic, he had money. And I know of countless others locked just as tragically inside prisons of their own making. They have grossly abused their accounts in the Bank of Acceptance. Stubbornly demanding their own happiness through irresponsibility, they have sentenced themselves to a hellish solitary confinement.

The mind God has given you and me is a marvelous thing. Through the conscious employment of that mind he effects in us the changes he wants. Looking again at Romans 8, we see the repeated emphasis on setting the mind on the Spirit. Later in 12:2, Paul returns to this key principle, saying that we must not opt simply to be conformed (literally molded) to this age or world. Rather, he says we are to be transformed (literally metamorphosed) by the renewal of the mind. Phillips' rendering is especially vivid:

> *Don't let the world around you squeeze you into its own mold, but let God remold your minds from within, so that*

you may prove in practice that the plan of God for you is good, meets all his demands and moves toward the goal of true maturity.

Paul also tells the Ephesians (with essentially the same message to the Colossians) that putting on the new self is a matter of being "renewed in the spirit of your mind."[51]

In some circles a debate rages about the precise definitions of and distinctions between the so-called conscious, subconscious and unconscious mind. Some participants in the debate even argue against the actual existence of the subconscious or unconscious. In the closing pages of this chapter we will be using those terms but without addressing any of the technicalities or controversies about them. At the very least, they are useful metaphors that give us language with which to discuss the workings of the human mind. How much more we can say beyond that, I don't pretend to know. But imagine one more picture with me, that of a three-story house. The basement of that house is the Unconscious, the floor where old Image dwells. On the next floor, the Subconscious, is we find the library of stored Memory and Habit. And on the top floor is the Conscious living room of Action and Attitude.

Old Image sends messages up the elevator to the Subconscious. Typically, the messages say, "You are flawed. You are bad. You are doomed to repeat the same mistakes again and again. You are inadequate. You are condemned!" These impulses are passed on up from the Subconscious floor to the Conscious, as old Memories and Habits dictate Actions and even Attitudes. But is that the whole story? Does the process stop there? Whoever heard of an elevator that only goes up?

There is a down button on that elevator. If you want to create a habit, you begin with the attitude, the conscious decision to take the required action. And what molded old Image in the first place? Is it really true that the Image is permanently, irrevocably fixed before age six (or even in infancy, as some claim)? No doubt it is quite firm by then, even unlikely to change. But countless times God has proven his ability to do some very unlikely things with lives and minds that have been surrendered to him.

---

51   See again Ephesians 4:22-24 and Colossians 3:1-17.

The missing link in this Image-Habit-Action-Attitude chain—the needed "down button," if you will—is a Conscious counterpart to the Unconscious Image. This counterpart needs to be something just as powerful but also consciously observable and controllable. God has provided that something; we call it not Image but Imagination. Consecrated by God, Imagination can be the most powerful part of the mind.[52] It can be set on things above, on things unseen, on things of the Spirit, on things of the Christ within. It can employ the eye of faith, envisioning the new self from God's perspective. The heaven's eye view of the disciple is one of imputed righteousness and perfection. God sees what will be when he is finished because when he looks at you and me, he sees his Son and the finished work of the Cross.

By engaging the Christ-Centered Conscience with its ability to imagine, we now can override the self-defeating patterns generated by old Image and its Habits. We don't have to stay in the basement. We can start on the top floor with the Imagination, allowing it to determine the Attitude and allowing the Attitude to dictate the Action. Any consistently repeated Action will, in turn, become Habit. And over time through the sanctifying power of God's Spirit, that Habit can begin to soften old Image and remold it into the very Image of God!

In Romans 7:15-23, we read of a Paul who cannot do anything righteous even though he wants to. But in Philippians 4:13 there is a Paul who can do everything through the One who gives him strength. The one

---

52 Some Christians have been taught to distrust imagination, equating it only with the more devious and carnal machinations of human consciousness. Some have written it off as a tool only of ungodly, even demonic religions that should have no part Christian thoughts. This tragic mistake is due first to the mentality that says if others employ it, we have to avoid it. But that attitude overlooks the simple fact that imagination is God's creation. He had a righteous purpose for it long before humans found perverse uses for it. The controversy is due second, to an unfortunate translator's bias against the term "imagination" in some versions of the Bible. Whenever certain words for the human capacity to muse, to meditate, to think creatively, abstractly, futuristically, etc. were found in positive, godly contexts, English renderings such as "meditation" were used. Only when these *same words* described sinful thoughts did the rendering, "imagination" occur. It is, therefore, inaccurate to claim that the Bible speaks of imagination only in negative ways. It is the translating that creates such an artificial distinction, one that simply does not exist in the original. At any rate, our working definition of the word "imagination" is nothing more than that God-created capacity to think creatively and postulate different possibilities, abstractions, and ideals. The fact is, humans cannot not imagine.

difference is the One who gives the strength. But Paul, does the change all take place overnight?

> *I do not consider myself to have "arrived," spiritually, nor do I consider myself already perfect. But I keep going on, grasping ever more firmly that purpose for which Christ Jesus grasped me.*
>
> *Philippians 3:12 (Phillips)*

Accounted perfect while being made perfect. Our Father is the artist who sees the complete masterpiece within the first stroke of his brush. He urges us on with confident love, saying, "I know you can do it because I can do it and I am at work in you!" He positions us at the starting block and shouts, "Get ready! Get set! I proclaim you the winner! GO!"

We begin just as we began learning to walk or ride a bike or drive a car. Our initial inadequacy is so great, we don't even know that we *are* inadequate. Then we are nearly overwhelmed by the growing realization of that inadequacy but we push on in faith—cautious, halting and inconsistent though we may be. But adequacy slowly builds—from one degree of grace-granted glory to the next. Eventually, this new way even starts *feeling* right—as if it actually fits—until one day we wake up actually *feeling* like Christians, *feeling* loved by God, *feeling* that full Acceptance!

Please understand, that feeling may be long in coming. In fact, it comes and goes only to come and go again! So John reminds us to go ahead and act like true disciples whether we feel like it or not. We don't have to wait for the emotion to make the decision. Right now, and at any time, we can put love into action, even when the old messages are telling us it's all a sham. Why?

> *Because this is how we know that we are coming from the truth, and how we, in his company, calm the doubt in our heart whenever our heart would condemn us. For God is greater than our heart, and he knows all!*
>
> *I John 3:19-20*

Isn't that amazing? He really does know all about my emotional, wavering, self-damning heart. He knows the struggle I have with old Image. At times, its pursuit seems almost relentless: "Who do you think you're fooling? You're no Christian! You are the same selfish, loveless, hopeless, pathetic failure you have always been!"

But now Christ has engaged the struggle; "the battle belongs to the Lord."[53]

Can it really be so wonderfully true? Not only does God know how I feel but he knows *why*—even when I don't! And he knows the solution; he knows the greater and final truth of my identity and my salvation. He understands even when no one else does; even when I can't. And wonder of wonders, *he* comes to set me free!

So when that "saved feeling" strays away for awhile, I needn't despair. I needn't doubt that salvation, for it is based on something—on Someone— far greater than a feeling. As incomprehensible as it may *feel,* in Christ I *know* who I am and where I stand in God's sight. And I am learning to trust his unchanging promise rather than my own erratic emotions.

> *That is why we don't become despondent. But even though our outer person is deteriorating, our inner person is being renewed daily; because this immediate lightweight adversity will be far more than outbalanced by the heavyweight glory it is producing for us. So we focus not on the things that are actually visible, but on the things that are invisible, because visible things are temporary; invisible things are eternal.*
>
> *II Corinthians 4:16-18*

---

53 I Samuel 17:47.

PART THREE

The Body
of
Christ

CHAPTER SIX: "...TO THE LEAST OF THESE..."

But you are a chosen race, a royal priesthood, a holy nation, a people for God's possession so that you can broadcast the excellencies of the One who called you out of darkness into his marvelous light.

I Peter 2:9

Tom and I had had several conversations over the weeks. I thought we were pretty well acquainted. I had already asked him about his family and he had mentioned his brother. The first name was somewhat unusual; paired with their last name it was downright unmistakable. And even though I had just seen the brother star in the biggest motion picture of his career, it still didn't register for me. We weren't in Hollywood; we were in Texas. Tom wasn't a celebrity; he was, in the vernacular of the region, a good ol' boy. He was unaffected, down home "regular people." Why in the world would I have connected him with a movie star?

But on this particular day Tom was telling me about a family reunion he had attended the week before. He mentioned in passing how glad he was that his brother had been able to finish a location shoot just in time to attend. Suddenly, it dawned on me who his brother was and I felt rather silly. Tom had probably thought I was unusually blasé when he first told me his brother's first name. And now it was a little late to say, "Wow! Can you get me an autograph?" But the silliest thing of all, I'm ashamed to admit, was the fact that I caught myself feeling different about Tom!

Has anything like that ever happened to you? Do you know anybody that's related to *some*body? Who is the biggest celebrity you personally know? The highest ranking official? The wealthiest, the best looking, the most powerful? Do you know any royalty? Do you have any famous relatives? My aunt, the genealogist, tells me we're descended from Lord and Lady Godiva. When you are in the presence of celebrity, do you feel somehow different—awestruck or awkward, fawning or fainting, even affecting a nonchalance that refuses to be impressed? Or have you ever experienced the presence of a greatness that somehow brings out the best in you?

You've heard the charge many times, "People go to church just to see and be seen." No doubt that is true in some instances but those who seem to say it most are those who may not have investigated enough to know. Furthermore, this over-generalization is often accompanied with another, "All Christians are so judgmental." The critics never seem to catch the irony of their own self-indictment. Nevertheless, at the risk of giving them more ammunition, would you go to church with me just to see whom we can see?

Do you see any celebrities? Any movers and shakers—or merely the shaken? How many of these people are a little too old for your comfort? Too young? Too rich? Too poor? Too dark-skinned? Too light-skinned? Too traditional? Too progressive? Good grief, who are these people?

But wait—we forgot to put on these glasses. They have very special corrective lenses. When you look through them into a mirror you say things like this: "It is no longer I but Christ." And when you look through them at other disciples you find yourself saying, "It is no longer *you* but Christ." These are the bifocals of self-denial/Christ-realization. The first field of vision sees "no longer I but Christ." The second field sees "no longer you but Christ." We can call these two fields "first-person self-denial/Christ realization" and "second-person self-denial/Christ-realization."

For you and me to see really where we are and who we are with, both first- and second-person self-denial/Christ-realization are critically necessary. Now we can see beyond our *I* issues, the fears, the questions, the weaknesses, the biases of self. Moreover, we can see beyond the *you* issues, the fears, questions, weaknesses, biases and the *differences* in those other selves. Glasses on? Then let's look again...

Why, is that a holy woman I see? And isn't that man a priest? Look, we're surrounded by royalty! We're in the company of saints, not marble myths but flesh and blood saints.[54] These citizens of God's Kingdom are, in fact, ambassadors of the King.[55] These princes and princesses are heirs of the Kingdom, co-heirs with Christ![56] Don't let the flesh disguises fool you; these are beings of light, of purity, of power. Don't let the number of wrinkles mislead you; every one of these new creatures[57] is younger than an infant and older than Methuselah. They are timeless; they are eternal. For these are the very children of God. These are your sisters; these are my brothers.

We've gone to Church, you see—not a building of wood or stone, not a program that takes up one hour a week—but to Church, to Zion, to the Temple of God. These are the Chosen People, and every one of them has received adoption into the Family, ordination into the Priesthood, election into the Kingdom, incorporation into the Body, and an invitation, blood engraved, into the Royal Banquet![58]

You are far enough along in this book that you already may have identified repeated stylistic idiosyncrasies of mine that annoy you. What if, as you get to know me better, you find more and more of my habits and characteristics to be downright off-putting, even disgusting? What if you decide that you don't like me at all, that I am generally wrong-headed and offensive? Could your view of me become so severe that even my virtues look to you like vices? Could I, in your eyes, do nothing right even when I am, in fact, doing right? What would you do with me? What if you had to work or worship with me?

I pray you and I could never get to that point with each other but I confess to having had those kinds of thoughts and feelings about other people. Can you think of someone right now that you find just that unattractive? But then, what if you could see past all that alienates you and that person? What if God gave you the grace to apply second person self-denial/Christ-realization even in this instance? What if—just imagine—you actually could see the being that God is re-forming from one degree

---

54 See Romans 1:7, one of dozens of New Testament passages that use the word "saint" not in reference to an elite group of super-Christians but to all disciples.
55 II Corinthians 5:29.
56 Romans 8:17.
57 II Corinthians 5:17.
58 See Luke 14:15-24; Romans 8:15-17; Galatians 4:6; Ephesians 1:22-23; 2:21-22; Hebrews 12:22-24; I Peter 1:1-2; 2:2-10; Revelation 19:9; etc.

of glory to the next? What if you could literally see the finished product? Suddenly it's not a matter of merely tolerating that character. Suddenly it is all you can do to resist falling down and worshipping that glorious being![59] Paul put it this way:

> *So from now on we view no one from a merely human perspective; In fact, we once looked at Christ in the merely human way, but no longer is that the way we know him. So then, with anyone in Christ, you have a new creature. The old things have passed on by. Now look: they've become new!*
>
> *II Corinthians 5:16, 17*

Jesus himself said it with the most dramatic simplicity: "I tell you that just as surely as you did to any member of my family, even the least, you did to me" (Matthew 25:40).

Now we understand why the New Testament places so much emphasis on *koinonia,* the fellowship of the saints. This sharing, this participation, this partnership, this getting together (in the deepest sense) is far more than the optional icing on the cake of discipleship. Fellowship is essential because in each brother and sister Christ takes on concrete reality.

You and I are family. We are the church. Whenever we come together, we come, not as two selves but as members, organs of the one body of Christ. If that is true then I will approach you in a state of first person self-denial/Christ-realization. I am not here to increase or protect my status within this fellowship. I am not here to promote my agenda. I am here simply to be Jesus to you. I am the vessel, the clay jar; Christ is the content.

I embrace you, then, from the perspective of second person self-denial/Christ-realization. I honor the Christ in you, the one reality that, for me, eclipses every detail of your mortality. I see your immortality.

Because we both are being transformed by Christ, we don't have to remake each in our own images. We can afford those differences of taste, perspective and disposition that might otherwise become barriers between us. Indeed, we can celebrate our distinct gifts, talents and personalities,

---

59 This thought is inspired by writings of C. S. Lewis. See especially *The Weight of Glory,* Grand Rapids, Michigan: William B. Eerdmans Publishing Company, 1965, pp. 12-15.

all subject to our sovereign Lord.[60] We show, not passive or indifferent tolerance, but active and invested love.

We hold each other accountable, not to our own human standards, but to the Lordship of Christ. And seeing by faith the Christ in each other, we graciously call forth that Best from one another. Like the eye and the ear of the body, we allow each other the freedom to operate as independently as necessary to fulfill our given functions. But like that eye and ear, we cooperate selflessly for we share the same lifeblood. We share one Head.

As I draw closer and closer to Christ, as I by the power of his Spirit I keep holding fast to the Head[61] and as you draw closer and hold on to him, too—what happens to the distance that was between you and me? Paul insists, "There is no longer Jew or Greek, no longer slave or free, no longer male and female because you all are one in Christ Jesus" (Galatians 3:28).

We slowly come to comprehend ourselves as living parts of the Body with Christ as our Head. As the gap between us closes, we turn our gaze upward, not as much face to face as shoulder to shoulder. We look up to that glorious Head. This discovery of who we are reveals to us another facet of self denial/Christ-realization. It isn't exactly first person plural; we might best designate it *corporal* or even *corporate* self-denial/Christ-realization.

The church is not a confederacy, a collective or a corporation (as the term is usually understood) but a *corpus*—a living body. She is—we are—literally "Jesus Christ, Incorporated." Corporate self-denial/Christ-realization, then, is nothing more nor less than the church knowing and being just who she is.

The church is herself only to the degree that she continually turns out from herself in order to look solely to Christ. If she is truly a church *of Christ*—and not just another church *of church*—she will deny all egocentricity of organization and mission. She will then continue to realize a fuller, deeper involvement in the ministry of Christ to the world. Her only agenda will be his agenda; her only power, his power; her only way, his way; her only righteousness, his righteousness; her only glory, his glory. Christ is all and in all![62]

---

60 Romans 12:1-8; I Corinthians 12:1-31; etc.
61 Colossians 2:19.
62 Colossians 3:11b.

We are called to be the body of Christ, and make no mistake about it, that body is a wounded body, scourged, pierced and vulnerable. We are not in the business of self-preservation. We are in the ministry of sacrifice. It is not only the individual disciple but the church as a whole that must be ready to be poured out like sacrificial wine upon the altar. As John the Baptist was the Elijah, the herald, of Christ's first coming,[63] so the church must serve as the Elijah of his second coming—even if that means that we, too, must decrease that he might increase.[64]

Too long and too often, we have used claims of stewardship and expediency to justify an increasingly vested interest in *our* real estate, *our* resources and *our* position. It is time to repent, to surrender the church to the only One who can make her a living, unified Body.

I suppose such statements have become clichés in some circles. And I know that such talk can be used as an excuse for abandonment of responsibility, poor stewardship and lazy discipleship. The book of Acts, however, tells of a truly surrendered church that was, because of that surrender, all the more active, diligent and creative. Cliché or not, the church and her individual members must "let go and let God," and one sure sign that they have done so will be radical, resourceful, responsible obedience.

Like Israelites led by cloud and fire, the church must let the Lord lead when and where he will. Then we find ourselves in the place he wants at the time he wants. We proceed only because He says to proceed. We wait only because He says to wait. Without corporate self-denial/Christ-realization, even our best efforts will be only so much busyness of the flesh. But with Christ in control, any endeavor is the business of the King!

For some years now, I have carried an image around in my head; I think of it almost as a vision. It is difficult to describe but I can't seem to think about corporate self-denial/Christ-realization without its symbolism coming to mind: It is the Lord's Day, the congregation has gathered, the pews are filled. Then something incredible happens. Everyone stands. As one body and to a person, they are swept with a glorious surrender and repentance. Their gaze is turned upward, away from themselves and their pews and their pulpit. At exactly that same moment, the roof of the church

---

63   Matthew 17:11-13.
64   John 3:30.

building is blown away as if by some fantastic explosion. And with hearts and hands and heads lifted to the heavens, they sing to their Sovereign, releasing all that they are and have to his Lordship. Then the walls of the now roofless building come crashing down. Brick and stained glass fall outward. No piece is left atop another. The church is able to walk out and be Jesus to the world. On the next Lord's Day, the very same thing happens as if it had never occurred before. And the next Lord's Day, and the next and the next, until one day the disintegrating of the roof reveals the Lord himself. And the congregation ascends to meet him in clouds of glory!

> *But you have come to Mount Zion, to the city of the living God, heavenly Jerusalem, to myriads of angels, to the grand gathering, the assembly of the firstborn who have been registered in heaven—to God, Judge of all, and to the spirits of the righteous made perfect, to Jesus, Mediator of a new covenant, and to the sprinkled blood that speaks more powerfully than that of Abel.*
>
> *Hebrews 12:22-24*

CHAPTER SEVEN: "...DISTINGUISHING THE BODY..."

But a time is coming, right now, when the real worshipers will worship the Father spiritually, authentically because that is exactly the kind of worshipers the Father seeks.

John 4:23

They sat in silence on their orange crate pew: Bunny Rabbit, Teddy Bear and my Cowboy Bob doll. I led singing from the pulpit—another orange crate, this one turned on end. "Bringing in the Sheets! Bringing in the Sheets!" Well, after all, I was only four. After another song, I passed a pie tin around. Mom had graciously supplied a soda cracker that I placed broken into the tin. And there was a cup of Kool-Aid to share with the congregants (at other times the tin and the cup were empty and we had to pretend). A short prayer, one chorus of "Marching to Zion," and it was time for the main event, the sermon. I let Bunny and Teddy and Bob have it with both barrels. When I got through with them, they knew they had been to church!

The tiny congregation wasn't that much smaller than the real country church of my childhood. Come to think of it, the levels of response and participation weren't totally dissimilar to those I've experienced since in a few live congregations. In fact, the more I reflect on it, the clearer it becomes: My little worship service missed the Biblical mark in many ways but, point for point, it symbolized frighteningly well what has sometimes passed for worship in the "real" world.

In the fourth chapter of John, Jesus discussed getting *real* with worship. He talked with the woman at the well about authentic worship offered in

Cruciform — in the shape of the Cross

68

spirit (and in Spirit) and truth. The coming of Jesus heralds the beginning of a return to Eden. With the fall came expulsion from Paradise and increasing complication of worship. Sacrifices had to be initiated. Altars had to be erected. A priesthood had to be formed. And finally a temple had to be built. But he degrees of separation between holy God and sinful humanity could not be fully overcome—not until He sent his Son.

The Cross perfectly and finally fulfills the old sacrificial system. Jesus brings down the curtain on the temple drama of continual blood offerings. The risen and ascended Christ raises up a glorious new temple to house the divine Presence; he builds us—you and me—into a sanctuary of *living* stones![65] And he sends us his own Spirit. Now the Shekinah, the very glory of God, dwells in and with us. Our liturgy, our worship service, consists of our daily lives, now sacrifices to our King.[66] And in that offering of ourselves to him, we find our greatest joy!

What happens, then, when the body comes together to celebrate the glory of its Head, Jesus? What happens in the assembly of the self-denied/Christ-realized? It is no longer I but Christ, no longer you but Christ, no longer our organization but his organism. So how do first person, second person, and corporeal self-denial/Christ-realization bear upon this thing called worship, particularly our corporate worship?

Suppose I ask you to write a paragraph titled, "The Ideal Worship Service." What would that paragraph say? Think back on conversations you have had or heard that began something like this: "Today's service was especially good, wasn't it?" Or like this, "I don't know about you but I didn't think much of that service today..." What followed those opening statements? What criteria were used to determine the success or value of the assembly? Doesn't it seem that the measuring stick is self? In fact, don't the conversations often begin, "I really got a lot out of the worship," or "I just didn't get much out of that one"? Who is this "I"?

I'm not suggesting that such remarks constitute terrible sin or that they have no place at all in the disciple's conversation. But maybe they reveal some mis-emphasis. Is "getting something out of it" the first and highest

---

65   II Corinthians 6:16; I Peter 2:4-10.

66   The New Testament consistently employs the language of temple ritual in a whole new way. For example, notice how *latreian* (religious service or worship) is used in Romans 12:1, or *leitourgia* (priestly service or ministry—the term is the source of our English word "liturgy") in Philippians 2:17.

goal of worship? And what is the "something" we are looking to get? Certainly, it must be more than mere entertainment or goosebumps. Surely, it goes beyond social-club camaraderie. Is it enlightenment and insight; is it encouragement and inspiration? Conviction, cleansing, communion? Those all are wonderful and important things but aren't they by-products of worship? The purpose of worship is worship: to offer glory, praise, adoration, thanksgiving, and honor be to God. The first question to ask of our assemblies is not what we get out of it, but *is God glorified?*

Wouldn't you know it, though, God has graciously arranged things so that worship inevitably is most refreshing and rewarding precisely when we lay aside self-oriented concerns and center our hearts first on his glory. So, even in worship we find yet another wonderful way that seeking is losing but losing is finding. Nevertheless, we will enter the sanctuary of praise, gladly ready to receive nothing other than the assurance that God is glorified.

Here is still another paradox: True worship is our selfless offering up to God. He is the Recipient, the Audience, the Beneficiary of all adoration and blessing. Yet, worship is very much God's own doing. Not content to be a passive receiver of our praise, He himself sanctifies and enlivens our offering by becoming the active Creator of all that is *real* worship, worship in the Spirit and in the Truth. God initiates and maintains the motion; we respond. Individually and corporately, we undergo the emptying of self that he transforms into our filling with his glorious Self.

We bow in prayer, and that prayer is powerful, not because we are great prayer-givers, but because God is the great prayer-Hearer. Indeed, through the unutterable intercession of his Spirit, God is the Producer of all *real* prayer.[67] Again we find ourselves, not so much the givers, but the responders. Be it prayer or praise, song or service, worship that is self-initiated or self-powered or self-seeking is always pitifully self-contradictory and self-defeating. But worship that transcends self to be given to, centered on and animated by God is blessing beyond compare.

In more ways than one, true worship must be cruciform; the Cross is the blueprint of our worship. The upright beam is the raising of our hearts and voices to God. The crossbeam is the pouring out of ourselves to each other in our shared love. Again, in his wisdom and grace, God has so

---

67   Romans 8:26-27 (see also Galatians 4:6).

arranged things that he accepts as worship the love and encouragement we give to each other. We ask first of our assemblies, "Is God glorified?" Then we ask, "Is the body edified?" This matter of "body building" was so important to Paul that he emphasized it directly or indirectly virtually every time he wrote about the assembly. It is the overarching theme of I Corinthians 11-14, the New Testament's longest single discussion of matters pertaining directly to the assembly.

In Chapter Ten, Paul has spoken already of the one body and one loaf which is the *koinonia,* that is, the sharing, the participation, the fellowship, the mutuality, the common union or communion in the body of Christ.[68] He has talked also of the need to do, not that which is merely permissible, but that which actually builds up others.[69]

In Eleven, then, he applies these principles of body *koinonia* and edification first to the way men and women conduct themselves in public prayer and prophecy. Then, he applies it further to the Eucharist, the meal of thanksgiving and remembrance. In Twelve, the application is to the use of spiritual gifts. There he says that even though the body has a great diversity of parts and functions, this diversity serves the unity of the one body. So the greatest gift and the most excellent way is that of the body-edifying, *koinonia*-enhancing love which Paul describes in Chapter Thirteen. Finally, in Fourteen, he comes back to the use of spiritual gifts. He calls for a protocol and a decorum that glorifies Christ as it edifies his body in that rich, loving *koinonia.* Again and again, Paul says, "It's not about you, the individual; it's about you all, the body—because ultimately it is about Christ, the Head!"

How often have you heard the question, "Can't I worship God alone at home or at the lake?" Of course I can, though reading the Sunday paper or reeling in that trout are likely to take precedence. But the question misses those key elements of edification and *koinonia,* the very things that makes corporate worship just as absolutely essential as private devotion.

At various times and places in the first century, disciples had all kinds of reasons to opt for the strictly private devotional. Beyond questions of personal taste and convenience, gathering with the saints could be dangerous, even deadly. Even so, for the writer of Hebrews, abandoning

---

68   I Corinthians 10:17.
69   I Corinthians 10:23, 24.

corporate worship simply was not an option. He said that we are responsible to each other; we are to inspire each other to love and good works. Therefore, it is imperative that we maintain this assembly habit as a fundamental means of mutual encouragement.[70]

In the assembly, I am afforded a special opportunity to show Jesus to you and to see Jesus in you. You and I, then, can visibly, tangibly *be* and *build* the body as we celebrate the Head of our glorious union. We can do that only *together*—and not just you and I but the rest of the family too. The younger ones, the older ones, the ones we agree with, the ones we think are confused. The assembly is where we physically demonstrate what we spiritually are: one body. And though the parts of that body have innumerable differences, they have one Head. He outweighs all the differences; his blood overcomes all that would separate us. That is our message to each other and to the world each time we come together in worship. No private devotion, regardless of how inspiring or transcendent it may be, can deliver that imperative message. Furthermore, if the fruit of my private encouragement isn't then brought to be shared with all the members, the body cannot be edified. My faith becomes an ingrown and selfish thing. Like a severed finger I can neither perform my function for the body nor receive life from the body.

Have I come full circle, then? Am I back to assessing the assembly on the basis of what I get out of it—simply rephrasing the question to read, "Was I edified?" I don't think so. Scripture calls me to take seriously my part in edifying *the body,* not myself. Once more, in God's gracious economy, the individual member of the body will best be filled up when the entire body is built up, just as the body is built up when the Head is lifted up in praise. But again, I must note carefully where the priority lies. When I do, I come away realizing that self-denial/Christ-realization is the authentic perspective on *real* worship, worship in spirit and in truth. When God is glorified first, the body will be edified best and thus I will be satisfied most.

How would you like to throw a party to honor someone we greatly love, admire and respect? We want to show our honoree just how special he is to us. Of course, we want to do this in a way, first, that he will enjoy and then, that will enable the happy and enthusiastic participation of all

---

70 Hebrews 10:23-25.

the guests. So, if we know he prefers dinner parties to costume balls, we'll make it a dinner party even if our personal preference is the ball. After all, we remember who the center of attention is and we've been to those embarrassing parties where that was forgotten; where the guest of honor was lost in the hubbub of competing egos. We want this party to focus on our honoree in a way that truly esteems him and joyously engages all the guests. We want everyone glad that they attended because, first and foremost, the honoree was appropriately celebrated.

Now, shall we have music? Yes, and not just any old music but songs that laud our guest of honor. Certainly, we'll include testimonials and stories about our honoree. Let's make time, too, for guests to visit with him and give him their gifts. And we certainly want him to have the opportunity to speak. Finally, of course, we want to have his favorite refreshments.

And for nearly 2000 years now disciples have gathered each Lord's Day, just as they did in the days of the apostles, to honor their God and Savior. They, too, sing songs of praise and they tell that story which never grows old. It's their story, yes, but his story first. They offer up prayers and gifts to their Lord. They listen as He speaks to them through his word. And they do indeed take refreshment: they celebrate Communion!

The Eucharist—the feast of Thanksgiving—may be the consummate expression of the nature of the Christian assembly. I understand that all elements of worship are important but, for me, nothing dramatizes more beautifully all the cruciform, Christ-in-me, Christ-in-you, Head-with-the-body reality of our worship than the Supper. This rite is, oh-so much-more than a cracker and some Kool-Aid. And it *is* real—no need to pretend with empty pie tins and cups.

It is the Lord's Supper—his, not ours. But we are the welcome guests. By the grace that makes us his body, the supper does become ours too.

It is the Lord's Supper. That adjective translated "Lord's" is very rare in the New Testament. It occurs only in I Corinthians 11:20 of the Supper and in Revelation 1:10 of the Day. It suggests not only ownership—the Lord's Supper—but even more, it connotes quality—the Royal Supper, the Regal Supper, the Imperial Supper, the Lordly Supper.

It is the Lord's Supper, a meal in which the Host is himself the Food. It is his body and his blood that we see in the bread and in the wine We receive his essence; he commingles his very self with ours. His presence in this supper is quite *real,* for the greater reality is not the physical but the spiritual.

What could only have been bizarre now becomes beautiful as ears of mere flesh give way to the hearing of faith.[71] What was "unscientific" is now undeniable—this certainty of the unseen.[72] What was intolerable heresy to the merely rational mind is now inescapable reality to the renewed mind. Holy Lord, let us never do ourselves the disservice of considering things spiritual as somehow less substantial. If physical things are substantial then spiritual things are super-substantial.[73] Everyday, as we see more of the physical fade and die, we come to admit that only the unseen is eternally real, the fulcrum of our faith.

It is the Lord's Supper. With his own life he confirmed the reservations to this banquet. We memorialize that sacrifice but we recall even more than a meaningful fact from history. This is a living memorial to a living Lord. In this meal, we remember the empty tomb and we claim his promise, "I am coming!" We celebrate the coming Lord who has come in the flesh, who comes again in the bread and the cup, who comes again in the brother and the sister, and who finally comes again to take us to the eternal banquet of heaven![74]

It is the *Lord's Supper.* He brings us into right relationship through his blood and condescends in love to be called *our* Lord. He invites us to his Supper, to his *koinonia,* his communion, his fellowship meal for his beloved.[75]

It is the *Lord's Supper* and that is why we see beyond the emblems to the *reality* they represent. As Paul phrases it in I Corinthians 11, we *distinguish the body of the Lord.*[76] We recognize the body that walked the dusty roads of Galilee, the body that gave up the Spirit on Calvary. But we distinguish, recognize, discern the body of Christ that still walks the earth and still enshrines his Spirit. We see the body that Paul has been talking about throughout that portion of his letter. We understand the

---

71 John 6 (see especially verses 51-55, 60-63, 67-69).
72 Hebrews 11:1.
73 II Corinthians 4:18, etc.
74 I Corinthians 11:26.
75 I Corinthians 10:16.
76 I Corinthians 11:29.

overwhelming *reality* that by the gracious power of his blood, we are no longer you and I. *We* are the very body of Christ. Praise God! Thank you, Lord Jesus!

PART FOUR

The Word

of

Christ

CHAPTER EIGHT: "...IF THEY KEPT QUIET..."

I planted, Apollos watered, but God made it grow. So neither the planter nor the waterer is anything, only the growth-giving God.

I Corinthians 3:6-7

An uneven preacher. You know the type; their sermons can fluctuate between mere mediocrity and sheer majesty. This sermon started out sounding as if it would be far to the mediocre end of the spectrum. In a weary drone, he read Luke 19:28-40, the "Triumphal Entry." By the time he finished the reading, he had begun to lose members of his audience—and he hadn't even started preaching yet! Suddenly, before anyone had time to focus on the starter pistol that had just appeared in his hand, the preacher pulled the trigger!

The bright, angry POP, instantly followed by startled screeches, reverberated through what had been a sleepy little hall. Brother Bud Grister reddened with compounded alarm as he heard echoes not only of the pistol but of the expletive that had escaped his own mouth. Sister Bertha Hunsbitter fainted dead away. Her husband managed to catch both her and the preacher's eye at the same time. That glare informed the young minister that this might well be a moving sermon—the week after it's preached, the preacher will be moving.

But what's a man of God to do when he has a vital message straight from God's word? The people need to hear it; they need to understand. But they act as if they have heard it too many times. They think they understand it all too well.

The Bible tells of prophets who sometimes resorted to starter pistol tactics. Jeremiah wore a big yoke everywhere he went;[77] Ezekiel shaved off all his hair and beard;[78] Isaiah went stripped and barefoot for three years![79] They were as dramatic, even bizarre and outrageous as necessary, employing arresting symbols of their crucial messages.

In that tradition, Jesus has arranged for an unforgettable final entry into Jerusalem.[80] It cannot be ignored, its prophetic significance cannot be mistaken. It is an event charged with symbolism, emotion and controversy.

It is the last Sunday before the cross. Every Sunday after will be radically, gloriously different. Jesus' disciples put him on a colt saddled with their own garments. This is an unmistakable parallel to the anointing of Solomon, son of David.[81] Now Jesus is riding the colt on Bethany Road into Jerusalem. As he comes over the ridge at Mount Olive, he can see the southeastern outskirts of the city and then, towering over its wall, the temple. He sees the crowd rushing to greet him and join with all the pilgrims that have already enlarged his entourage.

They begin to carpet his path with the palms waved in Passover worship. Then, they line his way with their own cloaks just as the people had done for another deliverer-king long ago.[82] Jehu had delivered Israel from evil Ahab; will Jesus now deliver Israel from evil Rome? Or are some in this crowd is looking for an even greater deliverance?

This is a bold and literally death-defying act on Jesus' part. After all, it is Passover. There are hundreds of thousands of pilgrims; they, along with the city's own large population, are filling Jerusalem to the bursting point. Anticipation and emotion permeate the very air. Pilate and his troops are nervous. And now Jesus is here to offer himself formally, one last time, to Israel as her Messiah, her King. This is his clearest public claim to messiahship yet.

His critics think it is, indeed, clear—clearly brazen, blasphemous, and unforgivable. They know what Jesus is doing. They know what this

77   Jeremiah 27-28.
78   Ezekiel 15:1-4.
79   Isaiah 5:1-3.
80   See Matthew 21:1-11; Mark 11:1-11; Luke 19:28-40; and John 12:12-19.
81   I Kings 1:32-40.
82   II Kings 9:13.

outrageous parade is suggesting. "King indeed! With all these impressionable commoners getting so stirred up, we're going to have a riot on our hands. And this time Rome's reaction may crush Jerusalem once and for all!"

But this is the gentle and humble King who rides, not the horse of military conquest, but the donkey of peace.[83] Perhaps they are right who call this the "Royal," rather than "Triumphal," entry. It comes, not after Jesus' victory, but just before his last great battle. And at the climax of that battle, the very moment of total defeat will be the actual point of *the* great victory over evil. Soon, the earth will quake and the veil of the temple will be torn from top to bottom.[84]

But the rending will not stop at the bottom of the veil. In the same way rocks were split, that fissure will somehow rip all the way down to the very bowels of hell. Satan and his minions will be opening their disgusting mouths and shaping their vile lips for cries and cackles of victory just as the cleft slashes through each of them. The deafening sound that will spew from their mouths is, instead of a victory cry, the most hideous scream of utter devastation and damned defeat the cosmos has ever heard!

These palm-waving pilgrims can't begin to know just how soon and how mightily God will respond to their shouts of "Hosanna!" A messianic cry that literally means, "Save now," it has become an exclamation that at once embodies the petition, the proclamation and the praise. Here at the outskirts of Zion, and at the outset of Passover, the celebration of an ancient deliverance become the exuberant anticipation of a new deliverance.

Psalms 113 through 118 were always recited at Passover, but now they are taking on a new and glorious and fuller meaning. More and more of the people pick up the shout of Psalm 118:26, "Blessed is the One who comes in the name of the Lord!" "Hosanna to the King! Hosanna to the Son of David!"

Messiah!

The startled stares of the members assured the preacher that he now had their full attention. From children poised with crayons in mid-air to seniors clutching their cough drops, the motionless crowd was transfixed. But then the preacher paused... And paused... Where was he going with this?

---

83   Zechariah 9:9.
84   Matthew 27:51.

Finally he spoke: "So what's the first thing that comes to your mind when I say the word, 'evangelism?'"

As far back as I can remember, I've been hearing pleas for more "soul winning." Some were harangues that suggested I wouldn't get into heaven unless I showed up with my quota of converts. Some were one-size-fits-all sales pitches for the latest gospel marketing gimmick. One must have started out as an outline in one of those sermon cookbooks because it surely did show up in a lot of different pulpits. Its dubious exegesis of John 15:2 claimed that fruit-bearing was nothing more nor less than soul winning. And we all know what happens to branches that don't bear fruit.

Most of those pleas left me feeling guilty, frustrated and sometimes defensive. A few increased my motivation, temporarily. Still fewer left me better equipped to share the gospel. Almost all of them made me wonder how I could achieve a healthier perspective on this issue. Surely, it involved more than a get-with-the-program-or-else mentality. Certainly, numbers cannot be the only criteria. Even hucksters and heretics can produce impressive headcounts.

When I realize how many wrong reasons and ways there must be, I feel almost paralyzed: by guilt; by pride and self-righteousness, by thoughts of trying to earn my salvation or trying to prove something as a "headhunter for Jesus." Method can consume the message; worse, it can pervert the message. Spiritual persuasion can lapse into carnal manipulation. The whole thing can become a competition of numbers and status between churches and individual Christians. Just how many ungodly games have been played in the name of evangelism? In fact, why, these days, does the very word "evangelism"—telling good news—sound like bad news to so many? Maybe I'll just stay home and read my Bible.

Still, there is something fundamentally off-center and out of kilter, something almost absurd about a disciple who has heard over a thousand sermons, who has sung over ten thousand hymns, who has read nearly a million words from that Bible of his, but who has brought zero persons to Christ. What could be more contradictory than a non-evangelistic Christianity? But does that mean that everything which passes for evangelism is Christian? Is it true only of the ancient Pharisees or is it possible that we, too, could travel land and sea to get a single convert, only to make him a child of hell?[85]

Again, I am confronted with the necessity of self-denial/Christ-realization. Evangelism isn't about me. I'm not out to alleviate my guilt, earn points or add stars to my crown. I'm not trying to prove my evangelistic prowess or rack up record-breaking figures for myself. In short, *I* am not out to do anything, *Jesus* is. He said, "For the Son of Man came to seek out and to save the lost" (Luke 19:10). And, "As the Father has sent me, I also send you" (John 20:21b).

It really is as simple as that; *Jesus* is the Seeker, the Savior and the Sender. The pressure is off me. I am a seed pouch, a watering can; I am a vessel.[86] God fills the vessel and God produces the fruit. Yes, there is a decision to make, but it's the decision to let Christ use me. Yes, there is work to do but it is Christ's work as He makes his power and his truth shine out from me. Gone, then, is the multitude of external or neurotic motives. In their place is simple commitment to the fact that evangelism is the business of Christ, and it is no longer I who lives but Christ in me.

Along with the proper motivation and purpose for evangelism, self-denial/Christ-realization also ensures the right perspective and content. When our human minds take over, first principles somehow start to get crowded out by secondary issues. Evangelism is reduced to debate over theological fine points and parochial concerns. These may have their places but only one thing stands in first place: Jesus Christ and him crucified![87] Jesus himself warned against that all-too-human ability to research the minutiae of scripture only to miss the One to whom it all points.[88] In Christ alone we have life. The signpost directs us to the Holy City. May none ever lose their way while we are arguing over the lettering on the sign.

Evangelism: telling good news. As individual Christians and as the body of Christ, we must practice a self-denied/Christ-realized evangelism if it really is to be *good* news at all. And along with first-person, second-

---

85 Matthew 23:15.
86 I Corinthians 3:6.
87 I Corinthians 2:2.
88 John 5:39.

person and corporate self-denial/Christ-realization, there is a third-person application that is critical to the good news mission.

It's so natural, isn't it, to view unbelievers as opponents, dangerous characters to fear and avoid? But what if you and I began to see them, not so much as enemy soldiers, but as prisoners of war? The mission of Jesus is neither a search and destroy maneuver nor, at the other extreme, a defense operation barricading the church against the onslaught of the world. His mission is nothing less than a rescue mission to set the captives free.[89]

When you and I talk about "them," what if we talked, not in terms of their hostility toward us or the threat they represent, but in the *seek* and *save* and *serve* language of Jesus? What if we saw past their relative goodness or badness, color or class, desirability or unseemliness, dullness or unresponsiveness? What if we saw past all the seemingly insurmountable barriers between us and those prisoners? What if we saw nothing but the potential reality of Christ within them? What if our imagination let us see them looking at us through the bars of a bamboo cage, their souls' true faces full of fear and pain? They bear such a strong resemblance to their Father, though still in captivity… What if, suddenly, we saw nothing but the potential reality of Christ within them?

We would then seek first to understand them before insisting that they understand us and our message. We would really listen as they express their doubts, their fears, their needs, even their anger. We would hear them cry out against injustice and we would respond. We would, with our Master, proclaim *good* news to the poor, liberty to the captives, sight to the blind and freedom to the oppressed.[90] We would get sweat on our brows and dirt under our nails as we live out before them God's justice and mercy, his help and his healing.

We wouldn't need so much to show them where they are wrong as to show them Jesus, who can make things right. We wouldn't have to have all the answers but we could introduce them to our Friend who does. Rather than merely tell them that God really loves and genuinely cares, we could show them as we let God minister to them through us. Even fear of rejection would no longer be an issue.

---

89   Luke 4:14.
90   Luke 4:18 (quoted by Jesus from Isaiah 61:1, 2).

Defensiveness wouldn't get in the way because no oppositional selves—theirs or ours—are in the way. Self no longer whispers, "Don't say anything! You'll just look stupid. Do you want to sound like a fanatic? You're in enemy territory here; this calls for stealth, not vulnerability." Instead, we hear the whispers of Spirit-wind, "You have a treasure to share! You have a song to sing! You have a Love to give!" And then seekers wouldn't be so guarded; in place of an attack, they would perceive only the offering of a Gift.

In Chapter Six, we looked at II Corinthians 5:16 as it applies to our perspective toward each other. But Paul said that from now on we view *no one* (believer *or* unbeliever?) from a merely human perspective. He goes on to talk about ambassadorship and the ministry of reconciliation. Mustn't it be with the perspective of third person self-denial/Christ-realization that we, as Christ's ambassadors, share that message?[91]

In the same chapter we spoke of seeing in each other, not only the work in progress, but God's finished product. As footnoted there, C. S. Lewis develops this idea with startling clarity in his small book, *The Weight of Glory.* In the closing paragraph of his first chapter Lewis puts it this way:

> *There are no ordinary people. You have never talked to a mere mortal. Nations, cultures, arts, civilization—these are mortal, and their life is to ours as the life of a gnat. But it is immortals whom we joke with, work with, marry, snub, and exploit—immortal horrors or everlasting splendours.*[92]

Christ sees that horror, he knows that splendor. His response is the Cross. What is my response? Tomorrow I will encounter another human being. I will do so as myself or as a vehicle of Jesus Christ. I will see that person merely as another self or as an immortal who has just as much "right" as I do to come to the point of saying, "It is no longer I who live but Christ." Lord, give me your eyes; let me see the soul you see.

I really don't understand why Christ would condescend to entrust such a privilege to us, but he invites you and me to be his Hosanna People. Our very lives can be the petition, the proclamation and the praise that is

91 II Corinthians 5:18-20.
92 Lewis, p. 15.

Hosanna! Think of it, lives transformed into shouts of the celebration and witness, "Blessed is the King who comes in the name of the Lord!"

The entranced congregation watched raptly as the preacher pointed out three groups of people lining the road into Jerusalem. He stood before each imaginary cluster as he described its responses to the Royal Entry. The first reaction was open, testimonial praise. As the preacher described the invisible celebrants, his listeners could almost see their joyful faces and hear their glad shouts. As the preacher moved to the second group, his audience sensed their open, sanctimonious disapproval in the snarl, "Teacher, reprimand your followers!"

As he described the third group, the preacher's animated face sadden. Turning his gaze upon his congregation, he explained that the last category was the most incomprehensible response of all: safe, self-absorbed silence.

But Jesus said, "I tell you that if they kept quiet, the very stones in the road would burst out cheering!"[93]

You see, the Hosanna is inevitable. God will see to it one way or the other. One day every tongue will be compelled to confess that Jesus Christ is Lord.[94] But on this day you and I can let him make us his Hosanna People. He can give us power that overcomes our inadequate selves, and He can give us vision that sees beyond the resistant selves of those who so desperately need this good news.

And as we come to understand the full extent of that news, the word "good" seems to glow in its pure and glorious absoluteness. When we look on our Christ, we are suddenly and breathlessly enraptured. Our hearts swell to the bursting with the painful joy of being so loved. Our minds are engulfed, our sight is dazzled. *Jesus!* He makes his Triumphal Entry into our souls as we awaken each morning, remembering both who we are and whose we are. We carry the wonderful knowledge with us, eager to share our story, longing to tell someone of our Lord, our dearest love.

It's hard to believe, this Good News. The very idea that our old, dead self has been melted away and in its place is a beautiful new creature—it's almost too glorious to comprehend. "The Lord has done this, and it is

---

93 Luke 19:40 (Phillips).
94 Philippians 2:11.

marvelous in our eyes!"[95] We need to tell the story just to hear it again and again ourselves, savoring the delight of such thoughts spoken aloud. We re-believe, re-envision, re-learn the message as we become the selfless messengers of our Messiahs' Triumphal Entry into more and more hearts. We revel in their triumph as they discover that their surrender of self to Christ has made them, too, "more than conquerors."[96]

"We *have* heard the joyful sound: Jesus saves! Jesus saves![97] Will we take up the glorious Hosanna shout? *Now?*

Suddenly, the preacher's voice fell silent. God had been moving in this sermon. The congregation seemed to share one breath, and it was being held, as they sensed the nearing conclusion. Even so, when the preacher *whispered* the final question, it hit with just as abrupt a jolt as that opening gunshot:

"Or shall we listen for the stones?"

---

95   Psalm 118:23.
96   Romans 8:37.
97   The opening words of the famous song, "Jesus Saves," by Priscilla Owens.

CHAPTER NINE: "...A WAY THAT SEEMS RIGHT..."

"If you stay in my word, you, in truth, are my disciples; and you will know the truth, and the truth will free you."

John 8:31b-32

I was trying desperately to keep the balance. I wanted to understand Jim, to appreciate his perspective, to listen—really listen—with sympathy's ear. But I had studied this issue many times before. I was convinced that God's word was clear on the matter. Jim was just—may I say it?—wrong. This was one of the watershed issues that distinguished orthodox Christianity from heresy. Jim was *dangerously* wrong. Still, I struggled to remain open-minded and sensitive. I fought the urge to overwhelm Jim with proof texts or intimidate him with finely calculated syllogisms. At one or two points of near exasperation, I just felt like using truth as if were a holy baseball bat. "Lord, please control the impulse," I prayed silently.

On the other hand, I knew I must not abandon that truth or treat it as unimportant. "Lord, make me fully compassionate without compromising your word. Make me quick to listen and slow to speak." But when the time came for a response, could I find a way to be fully persuasive without resorting to harsh debate tactics? "Lord, show me that balance—help me speak the truth in love..."

But then Jim—who, by the way, first raised the issue a hand—leaned back in his chair and looked off into space. "I've decided that the Lord doesn't want me to discuss this any more. He revealed the truth to me personally; he has given me an understanding and a peace about it but he doesn't want me to argue the point any more. He will reveal it to you when he and you are ready."

And that was that. Oh, I agree with you that Jim's move was probably a signal of self-doubt, but that was no comfort. Winning an argument was not the point. I didn't want to prove him wrong and myself right. I genuinely wanted God's truth to prevail. But how do you counter personal revelations—especially when they include prohibitions of discussion?

At least Jim was convinced that he was right and I was wrong. That is, he acknowledged some standard of truth. Growing numbers of people these days reject the entire idea of any fixed or universal truth. No doubt, some will read the story of Jim and think us both too burdened with rigid ideas of what constitutes truth. It isn't so much that they deny the existence of truth. Rather, they see all truth as fluid, relative and subjective. They aren't at all unpleasant about it. Share the Good News with them and they won't call it preposterous. They won't say that you are mad—or even mistaken. They will smile and say sincerely, "That's really beautiful and I know that it is all quite true, for you, but it's just not right for me."

This is not just an arbitrary or rebellious mindset. Many serious thinkers in our society have been trained to see reality as a confluence of endless possibilities, with nothing fixed or permanent, and with rules that are meant to be reshaped as new information continually redefines the world around us. After, all, as newborns, we discover the world around us; we grow and we enlarge our perceptions of reality as it unfolds throughout our lifetimes. We discover rules, we outgrow some, we replace and refine others.

What of truth? Where do we look for it? You found your truth in Christ; she found her truth in Buddha; he found his truth in his navel—isn't it wonderful that we all found what is right for us? But is this what Jesus means when he speaks of truth? Does he entertain the idea of *a* truth in flux or *a* truth that may be one of many different, even contradictory truths? Or does he speak of *the* truth, one truth that can be heard, believed, followed and shared?

Do you remember Pirsig's cheerful old character in *Zen and the Art of Motorcycle Maintenance?* She was Professor Phaedrus' colleague, Sarah, who challenged him to go and teach those students "Quality." Quality,

Phaedrus would puzzle to himself.[98] Quality. Was there some great absolute against which to judge good and bad in literature and in life as well? Was there Truth with a capital "T"? If not, how could one teach Quality? How could one teach?

Deep down, we all do need to discover the rules, don't we? Doesn't that mean that there *are* rules? Not the rules that change with the times or the culture, or even the latest scientific discovery but timeless rules that all other rules, at best, merely reflect or approximate. The rules that forever govern the universe. God's rules. Truth—truth that was true before we discovered it, truth that remains true even after we reject it.

While truth may have a variety of personal applications, truth that, itself, changes with each person is something other, something less than truth. There may be myriad truths, many of them paradoxes, but ultimately they are not really contradictions. For example, at the moment I'm holding my coffee cup; I can tell you truthfully that it is nice and warm to my hand against the chill of this room. But in just a little while, it will be cool. So there are differing descriptive possibilities, but not independent, arbitrary bits of truth that take on substance when I encounter them, only to lose that reality when you meet them, or take on whole other realities when yet another person confronts them.

The warmth of my cup is just its temporal description, not its essential definition. It's a cup, not a rocket ship, no matter how much I want it to be a rocket ship or believe it is. The problem arises when we confuse temporal truth that describes changing nature with eternal truth that defines eternal nature. That's *the* truth, the singular, final, absolute truth. And that truth is found in the Person who said, "I am the way and the truth and the life."[99]

In vogue or not, honesty requires us to admit that, at some level, we recognize objective truth. And we have to admit that, at an even deeper level, the Truth that is Jesus does resonate. We may try our hardest to discredit or domesticate Jesus but somehow we know that can't just disregard him.

If self-denial/Christ-realization (first, second, third person and corporate) truly is our way, our life, then the remarkable claim of Jesus

---

98   Robert M. Pirsig, *Zen and the Art of Motorcycle Maintenance,* New York, Bantam Books, 1981. pp. 160-164.
99   John 14:6a.

takes on the greatest significance to us. Christ equates truth to himself! In Christ, the truth is personal but not in the sense of being a matter of individual, subjective understanding. The truth is personal because it is Person. And in that Person the truth is universal. "No one comes to the Father except by me."[100]

While this Person is personally knowable, his truth is objectively discernible. In other words, that truth is not subject to individual understanding; rather individual understanding must be subject to that truth. As we submit to Christ, we submit to truth. With self-denial/Christ-realization as map and the cross as compass for both our personal and corporate journey, we affirm the reality of that Christ-truth to which we surrender. We practice, we apply that Christ-truth to our lives. And viewing the results, we come to realize that his word, even to our limited intelligence, is the ultimate truth. No other map, no other compass can bring us to our Destination.

Am I preaching to the choir here? You and I and our fellow believers have been fairly clear on this matter when talking to unbelievers. But what kind of treatment does objective, absolute truth get within our own ranks—within my own life? Would I stand in judgment of the world's subjectivism while in fact I stand judged for my own? I may not preach that "all is relative," but what do I practice? Do I open the Bible so that Truth can confront me and my preconceptions or so I can draft truth into the service of my notions? Do I belong to the Truth or does truth belong to me?

The pendulum of mortal mind does swing, doesn't it? You and I have seen the tragic results of the arrogant dogmatism that claims an exclusive franchise on truth. Being convinced isn't the same thing as being right, is it? But there is a real danger of over-reacting. Must I forever postpone taking a stand for truth, fearing that my stand has to be biased? Being confused isn't the same thing as being humble, is it?

I must be careful not to fall for a false equation. I may not have it all figured out, but it does not follow that objective Christian truth is wholly unknowable. I am limited; God's truth is not. He has revealed that truth in such a way that, even as a child, I could enjoy degrees of belief and appreciation. Yet, in this life I will never plumb all the depths

---

100 John 14:6b.

or comprehend all the facets of divine truth.[101] Aspects of that truth defy human logic but I must not then conclude that God's truth is irrational. It may be supra-rational—more than rational—but *never less.* The failing is not in the objective reality of God's truth but in the finite human mind and the limitations of the rational process. None of this changes the fact that the truth has been divinely revealed and that, with varying degrees of personal understanding and insight, we can accept and agree with that truth. You and I might even be able to agree with each other *about* that truth.

The great temptation is to make truth *subject.* One generation makes it subject to sacred tradition. Truth suffers, so another generation seeks to correct the problem by making truth subject to rationalism. Still another subjects it to empiricism. Another, to mysticism. God's truth can, in fact, speak to and through tradition, logic, experience and mystery. However, to make that truth subject to any of these is to subordinate the mind of God to the mind of man—Christ-denial/self-realization! Error is no less wrong even when we pronounce it absolutely true. Truth is no less right simply because we do not see it or cannot grasp it.

In the motion picture, *City of Angels,* even Hollywood got that point, when the angel said, "Just because you don't believe in something doesn't mean it isn't true!"

But isn't it true that as humans we can never fully escape our subjectivity? We may see that there are objective truths and absolutes but we see even these through the filter of our own biases. So why not admit that as far as you and I and this mortal life are concerned, all is relative? That's why cartoon Calvin doesn't make new year's resolutions: "See, in order to improve oneself, one must have some idea of what's 'good.' That implies certain values. But as we all know, values are relative. Every system of belief is equally valid and we need to tolerate diversity. Virtue isn't 'better' than vice. It's just different."

We have to agree with Hobbes' reply, "I don't know if I can tolerate that much tolerance."[102] Relativism is a self-contradiction. It states in the absolute that there are no absolutes. It proclaims the independent (non-

---

101 See I Corinthians 13:9-12.

102 Bill Watterson, *Calvin and Hobbes,* January 2, 1995, distributed by Universal Press Syndicate.

relative) axiom, "All is relative." And it doesn't take long before the frothy, artificial meringue of relativism makes us all long for something solid to chew. The meringue looks beautiful piled atop that strawberry pie, but it tastes like nothing, gives you nothing, really. Sometimes the absolutes may be a little *too* strong for our palate, but they're always preferable to that sickening froth.

Even now, we are seeing the backlash as more and more people cry out for clear, simple, yes/no answers. Sadly, there will always be plenty of self-proclaimed messiahs ready to exploit our hunger for easy absolutes. "Just do exactly as I say and all your problems will be over!" But the fact is, embracing the proposition of absolute truth is not a quick-fix, easy way out for people who are too lazy to think. Not all the answers are simple; and the relative things *are* relative. There are greater and lesser goods—and evils. Truth is as simple *and* as complex as it needs to be. That's why Paul wrote not only about milk but meat, and also why, according to Peter, some of what Paul wrote was hard to understand.[103]

But even if we refuse to resign to the conclusion that nothing is knowable—that the froth is all there is—we still look for shortcuts. Relativism can't be the answer but rationalism was little better, so let's try *ir*rationalism! Or is that just trading one kind of imbalance for another?

I hear so many sincere and well-intentioned debates about ways in which to revitalize the church and make the gospel fresh and relevant for today. In fact, many of those debates have taken place inside my own mind. I go back and forth as I imagine my quest to make the church into a sinner-friendly and soul-seeking body, deeply spiritual and dynamic. Those are worthy goals, but the means and methods I sometimes entertain lead me into dangerous waters.

I know that I over-think things; what if thinking is my problem? What if I'm putting more faith in human intellect than in Jesus Christ? What if I really do suffer from the "paralysis of analysis," using my brain as a bunker against the danger of passion and caring? Wouldn't it be more courageous just to listen to my heart? And more authentic?

But what do I do with all those passages where Paul speaks of mindset and even transformation through the renewal of the mind?[104]

---

103 I Corinthians 3:2; II Peter 3:16 (see also Hebrews 5:11-6:3).
104 Romans 8:5-8; 12:1, 2, etc.

Intellectualism can be a problem, but the answer isn't anti-intellectualism. God created me with a heart *and* with a brain. I can't reduce my walk and my worship to merely "emoting before the Lord."

Maybe our misplaced faith is in scripture and history over Jesus and his grace; maybe we study the past rather than live in the present. Doesn't a preoccupation with history just weigh us down and keep us from living authentically here and now? Who cares whether or not Jonah was really an historical person? His story is there just to challenge me to jump the ship of my own security into God's sea of possibilities, isn't it?

Reading the existentialists did remind me that faith isn't just passive belief in things that happened two thousand years ago. Christian faith is an active, living thing that requires tough, personal, here-and-now choices. "Leaps of faith," yes, but not leaps past all our history, our collective story, God's true story. Not existential leaps into the dark abyss of absurdity but faithful leaps into the bright security of a Savior who really did walk out of his tomb.

But what about meaningless traditions? They make us look so outdated, and they really do get in my way!

There are no such things as meaningless traditions. They became traditions because believers at one time found meaning in them. Those that are of human origin are subject to limitations of time and culture. When they have served their purpose, maybe I can appropriately, respectfully and lovingly put them up on shelf of our history's treasures.

But before I dismiss them offhand, I would do myself a much greater service if I learn their history, their original meaning and purpose. I would better serve the church if I didn't assume, just because I can't find a tradition's meaning, that no one else can. The old hymn that make my teeth itch turns out to be profoundly encouraging to the sister in the next pew. It reminds her of who and whose she is, and how she got here. And the contemporary praise song that has meant so much to me for the last thirty years has now become one of the boring old standards to the next generation. In fact, I've lived long enough to see several of my own "brilliant innovations" age into another's "meaningless traditions."

Arguing with myself this way makes me feel like the old liberal who said he really knew only one thing, which was that he really couldn't know anything! I'm tired of all this so-called "epistemological humility." If I just stay open to the Holy Spirit, won't he reveal everything to me? Won't he take me into higher and higher levels of special insight and spirituality?

I do want to stay open to God's Spirit, absolutely. I want to stay filled with the Spirit but I know that the ancient heresy, Gnosticism, is still very much with us. To be honest, I don't want simply to know God. I want to know the unknowable things of God. I want to know more than ordinary Christians know. I need some sort of quick, easy bypass that will take me around the nights of God's silence, the days of my uncertainty, the ever-present chance that I might get something wrong.

I need unmistakable, instant and intimate access. I don't want the Spirit to speak to me through other people (especially ones I don't particularly like), life-circumstances, hard study, mistakes, silence… I want him to speak clearly, straight from his heart to mine. I want to be able to assume that if I feel something strongly enough, it must be from God. I want to be one of the insiders who know the secret things of God. And I want constant access to the *thrill*. Knowing that about myself, I must beware of the shortcuts. Beware of the certainty of all but Christ.

What if we really do deny ourselves (with our many and conflicting agendas) and acknowledge Christ who alone is the truth? What if we allow the standard to be his gospel rather than our goosebumps? What if we answer his call to look outside ourselves and our subjectivity to his truth, which frees us and gives us *balance?* What if we go back to his words and *really* read them? What if we determine to live by his words and not our wishful thinking?

Yes, as in generations past, we will be imperfect in this venture. Our contrariness, our culture, our carnality will still find their way into the equation. Good and honest people will still disagree. But we will be surrendered to and blessed by the corrective of that divine balance. Balance that fully engages both mind and spirit.[105] Balance that makes for a personal, dynamic faith without reducing Christianity to a purely experiential, sensual medium of self-indulgence. Balance that redeems us from the inadequacy that knows nothing and the arrogance that knows it all. Balance that can be expressed with feeling but, even when feeling flags, is affirmed in faith. Balance that from start to finish is all about Jesus but by grace allows his story to be our story!

---

105 I Corinthians 14:15.

The tale is told of two fellows who just couldn't agree on a certain matter. Finally, a mutual friend invited them to his house. When they arrived he greeted them on the front porch where he had placed three buckets of water. The first bucket was nearly freezing, the second was room temperature, and the third was almost scalding. One fellow was asked to submerge his hand in the ice water while the other placed his in the hot water. After several seconds their friend told them both to change their hands to the center bucket. "Is the water above room temperature or below?" he asked. The first fellow replied, "Above," at exactly the same moment that the second fellow said, "Below." Their friend opined, "Seems we could use a thermometer."

Proverbs 14:12 reminds us of life's bitter but inescapable lesson that even though a way may seem right, in the end it can be the way of death. And, oh, doesn't experience bear this out? But thank God that he hasn't left us to our own devices—to our *selves*—but, in Christ and his word, has given us the thermometer. And Christ is far more than a cosmic thermometer. He is not only the Standard of right, he is its very Source. His word is true, absolute and unfailing, for Jesus himself *is* Truth.

There are two songs I've known as long as I can remember. I'm sure I learned the words to *Jesus Loves Me*[106]first. But it probably wasn't too long before I was working on at least the chorus of *He Lives*.[107] The first tune is considered strictly a children's song. The second was not written primarily for children. I still sing them both, though. *You ask me how I know he lives/ he lives within my heart.* But if you ask me how I know that he lives within my heart, then with Barth[108] I must refer to the superior theology of the children's song: *Jesus loves me, this I know for the <u>Bible</u> tells me so!*

---

106 *Jesus Loves Me,* words by Anna Warner (1860), music by William Bradbury (1862).

107 *He Lives,* words and music by Alfred Ackley (1933), copyright renewed 1961, The Rodeheaver Co.

108 The story is told of the great twentieth century theologian, Karl Barth (1886-1968), an exceptionally prolific writer. A student asked him to summarize in a few words his massive body of theological writing. Barth was not a man of few words but according to the story, he rose to the occasion simply by saying, "Jesus loves me, this I know, for the Bible tells me so." This quotation is found, among other places, in Michael P. Green, ed., *Illustrations for Biblical Preaching,* Grand Rapids, Michigan: Baker Book House, 1989, p. 377.

CHAPTER TEN: "IF YOU LOVE ME..."

*Whoever loves me will keep my word, and my Father will love
them. Too, we shall come to them and make our home with
them. Whoever does not love me does not keep my words. And
the word you are hearing is not mine, but is the word of the
Father who sent me.*

John 14:23, 24

It seemed like such a beautiful dream—but so short-lived. What went
wrong? This was to be the dawning of the Age of Aquarius. "Love and let
love," was the credo. Wear a flower, have a toke, and love everyone— even
the "pigs." But make it a cool love. The world has had enough of that
controlling, evangelistic, absolutist love. Just be free and allow others the
same privilege. No hassles, no commitments, no worries. Hang loose and
be happy. Do your thing and let others do theirs.

A decade later, Janet and I paid our first visit to San Francisco. As
we toured the streets of Haight-Ashbury, once the capital of the flower
children, our friend described the great community effort that had gone
into rejuvenating the neighborhood. After so many years of being almost
abandoned, it was looking alive and habitable again. The original spelling
of *Haight* was almost restored in the residents' minds.

But maybe, just maybe, the reclamation should not have taken place.
Perhaps the boards should have stayed on the windows and the filth on the
sidewalks. Maybe we needed a visible and vivid reminder—a monument,
as it were—that would never allow us to forget the Love Generation that
sank into *Hate*.

Maturity → *No Longer I but Jesus*
Let Him Lead You.

L. E. Hall

Now another three decades have passed. Most of the hippies who survived the drugs and the diseases have been long since reassimilated into conventional society, a few even as far as Washington, D.C. But what lesson did we learn? Was the only change merely an abandonment of the dream? Is cynicism any better than naiveté? Is addiction somehow less destructive if the addict knows he has no hope of reaching nirvana?

At least the hippies thought they had a noble reason for dropping out; they had a vision. But since that time the dropouts have continued precisely because they see no vision—no hope. As we survey decades of moral and ethical famine in our land, can we feel any better that, in place of poor solutions, we were offered no solutions?

What went wrong? The same thing that continues to go wrong. The same thing that went wrong with the ancient Greeks, the Pharisees, the Gnostics of the early church and the clerics of the medieval church. It is what went wrong with the Victorians and with the Lost Generation, the modernists and now the post-modernists. Whether moralist, existentialist, conservative or liberal, apart from true self-denial/Christ-realization, any ethical or moral system is doomed to failure. Without Christ, we are sure to recreate one of the two ancient heresies, Antinomianism or Pharisaism.[109]

The Sheep Know the Sheppard and will follow.

Both are still saying (I) am in charge.

---

109 With you permission, we will use these two terms in their more popular, if oversimplified, senses. Antinomianism has the strict historical definition of that teaching which holds that law is non-binding for Christians since it is faith that saves. But often the term is used to refer to a more general lawlessness. That looser definition will apply here.

Likewise, Pharisaism is commonly understood to refer to that brand of self-righteous, loophole-seeking legalism Jesus so harshly denounced. If we come away with a one-dimensional caricature of the Pharisees, we may do not only them but the words of Jesus a great disservice. We must understand that, historically, the Pharisees were among the spiritual athletes of their day. More than that of the Sadducees and other such sects, their theology was remarkably close to that of Jesus. Of the major Jewish groups in the first century, the Pharisees may have been the most widely represented among the first converts to Christianity.

Undoubtedly many sincere, devout Pharisees observed their strict codes out of sheer gratitude to God. In fact, I rather wonder if Jesus took some them to task not because they were so heinously far from the truth but because they were so frustratingly close. I can hear the profound pain in his heart when he says, "Woe to you Pharisees!" But it is not a hopeless pain; these woes are cries of warning, the kind of passionate pleas one makes only to those one loves and values deeply. So while there may have been all kinds of Pharisees, we still recognize a certain Pharisaism that generally epitomizes the legalistic approach to morals and ethics.

Love's Law *Love your neighbor as I love you.*

Love is the fulfillment of Law

Love the Lord your God with all your Heart, soul, and Mi—

98

We don't give in to Anger.

*What does Love Look Like?
I need the Holy Spirit
I need examples to follow*

No Longer I

A libertine and a legalist may seem to be at opposite ends of the moral universe but then, didn't Einstein say that the universe curves back in on itself? The Antinomian, says, "No law!" The Pharisee says, "All law!" But they both are saying, "Self is still in control." One rejects all codes, rules, laws and guidelines as arbitrary and overly restrictive, saying, in effect, "I will decide for myself, thank you very much, what and what not to do." The other would reduce righteousness to the observing of an exhaustive list of do's and don'ts: "Surely my fastidious observance of all the rules will earn me God's favor and humanity's gratitude."

Guess what? I can sing both those songs—almost at the same time! I can speak out against the evils I perceive in society both within the law and without. I can condemn unjust and arbitrary law that you try to impose on me while thrusting my own rigid expectations upon you. I can denounce a legalistic observance of the letter of law which results in a parody of the spirit of that law. But in the process, I can become just as self-righteous and judgmental as those I set out to correct. You're not going to tell me what to do, but let me tell you a thing or two!

My generation thought we invented love and brotherhood. To people once treated as subhumans we gladly cried, "Brother!" and "Sister!" But at the same time, to other fellow humans we were screaming a lot of other names unfit to print. Who more than our generation has had so much to say about love? But who more than our generation has tried to equate love with certain other four letter words that frequent our speech? Who before us was more vocal in objection to atrocity? But who before us was more atrocious in those vocalizations? We were right to call manipulation and exploitation obscene, but why did we have to use so many obscenities in the process? In truth, isn't it rather obscene that we—even in our highest courts—could never agree on a definition of "obscene?"

As long as our morality continues to be based in our humanistic pride, moral consistency will elude us. We will go on being bundles of self-contradiction, wildly judging each other while vehemently demanding that no one judge us. And we can forget about arriving at a consensus ethic. There is virtually no consensus in a society as pluralistic and tribalistic as ours. About the most we can hope for is some sense of political correctness, and who in their right mind would hope for that?

*carnal – un-surrendered law – I surrender All
works
carnal – un-surrendered Liberty –
Slavery
carnal – un-surrendered Love – Love one another
affections   with Pure love*

L. E. Hall

Even if true consensus were possible, history has proven repeatedly that such a consensus can be very immoral. When ethics are based on self and pride, all objectivity is lost. Things are no longer right or wrong, they are feasible or impractical, desirable or unappealing, agreeable or nonnegotiable. At that point, as Calvin (the cartoon, not the Reformer) told us in Chapter Nine, "Virtue isn't 'better' than vice. It's just different." In time, the very concept of virtue and vice become meaningless, even in ones own tribe.

Well, good old western pragmatism will take care of that, won't it? With enlightened self interest we will arrive at a utility ethic that makes up in practicality what it lacks in nobility.

Again, both history and the current chaos answer with a resounding, "No!" But even if we could achieve this functional morality, we still would not have restored that virtue that reflects our Maker's image. My apologies to the animal rights activists, but we are more than colonies of ants or bees. They may function very efficiently but we are called to function divinely.

Moreover, if we do produce a merely *human* virtue, we can still come up with nothing truly righteous, only things that are more or less "lofty." And even that loftiness is an illusion. In the end we must admit that it is arbitrary and tentative—as absurdly impossible as a cartoon character reaching back to his own collar and lifting himself off the ground. In a utilitarian system of ethics, things such as loftiness, quality and truth change with each culture, each generation within that culture, and each special interest group within that generation.

In such a system, there can be no sin, only things that are, at least for a season, "beneath us," inexpedient, or at least politically incorrect. But at too many times and in far too many places, unspeakable atrocity has been deemed expedient—even correct. We've seen, haven't we, just how ignoble we can be in the expression of noble ideas? And history proves that, given the right set of circumstances, absolutely nothing is beneath us.

Maybe everything in this chapter and the last sounds to you like so much philosophical gibble-gabble about society at large. You might rightly wonder, "What does this have to do we me as an individual disciple?" But isn't society, after all, a collection of individuals? I would be foolish to think that my culture has not influenced me. Let's not waste our time in a judgment-fest about "them;" it is we who need to be reminded of the

Called not to a system, but to a Savior.
Then no a self-denied, Christ realized
obedience.

truth about Truth. The personal implications of all this are crucial, as the tragic story of Jake will illustrate.

During that critical year of change, I was able to observe him perhaps more closely than anyone. Interestingly enough, it was during that same period of hippies and draft card burners. Jake had very little in common with such outrageous people. When I first met him, he was, in a word, cultured. He knew just what to say and just when to say it. He dressed and carried himself with about as much refined gentility as a fellow so young and inexperienced could muster.

Jake set high standards for himself and had exacting expectations of his associates. His use of profanity was limited to only the more sophisticated expletives; he would not tolerate the gutter talk and humor that other college men enjoyed. Habits that they thought harmless he viewed as base and disgusting. His high school records indicated a disciplined and highly developed intelligence. He had cultivated a talent in classical piano to a degree that ranked him with professionals and won him a full scholarship.

I wish I could tell you that all this was a response to the higher calling of God, that Jake had consecrated body, mind and talent to the glory of the Lord. But Jake wasn't even sure there was a god, and he was quite definite in his rejection of Jesus Christ. His only motivation was pride. He fancied himself above the low and bestial things of his peers. He believed that achieving ever higher levels of superiority was the most noble and worthwhile goal.

Be careful about dismissing Jake as an arrogant unbeliever. You and I both know just how easily such arrogance can infect the believer, too. In fact, we can compound the sin by labeling our pride as "godliness." There are few sins that drew any harsher condemnation from Jesus than that which he leveled against self-righteousness in professed believers.[110] Jake's story can come uncomfortably close to ours.

Now that Jake was away from home, there were new temptations. There were far more people who were unimpressed with his refinement. Of course, Jake had dealt before with what he called "the plebeian spite of the surrounding philistines," but these critics were different. They asked

---

110 See for example his parable in Luke 18:9-14 of the two men praying or, in Matthew 23, his seven woes against the Pharisees.

questions that Jake couldn't answer. "Who says your way is better? What constitutes loftiness or lowness? Why bother with self-improvement? What are you trying to prove? If self is god, then why not subject that self to every sensation and gratification? And if there is no god, it makes no difference, so why not do it anyway? Why not, Jake? Why not?"

The decline began subtly, with things one might have thought insignificant. But to Jake, even details of diet and hygiene were symbols of that fragile dignity he had built for himself. So when he became dependent on tobacco, the implications were far greater than a simple, common addiction. The same was true of his growing use of profanity and his new found love for perversely dirty jokes. Classes and homework became needless bothers. While several athletes made A's on the papers Jake sold them, his own grades plummeted.

The young man who, just months before, had only disdain for illicit sex was now using prostitutes. He found himself at parties where he could experiment with promiscuity and perversion. His new "friends" introduced him to hallucinogens and other street drugs. But his mind was already a horror house of bizarre images. With growing frequency he woke from nightmares that left him sweat-soaked and trembling. He would disappear for days at a time, reappearing with ever stranger tales. But by now it was impossible to know what Jake really was doing, for along with everything else, he had become a chronic liar who himself couldn't tell when he was or was not being honest.

One day Jake did manage to audition for an admired maestro, winning an invitation to spend the summer studying with the master and touring with him in concert. But even music, the thing Jake held dearest, was no longer worth the effort and discipline. He really didn't decline the offer, he just vanished again. The last I heard of him was a call from authorities trying to trace his whereabouts. The only trail they had discovered to that point was one of numerous bad checks. All this in less than nine months.

Why was I surprised? What happens to gardens untended, houses abandoned, sailboats left adrift in the storm?

What Jake lacked was a point of reference greater and truer than self. At the beginning of the school year some accused him of being too dignified. But what they were reacting to was not dignity, it was arrogance.

In fact, Jake never was truly dignified at all. Human dignity stems from the fact that we are created in the image of God.[111] We were made for his glory, and only in the fulfilling of that created purpose do we discover our own glory and dignity. The problem is that we all have sinned and have fallen woefully short of the glory for which we were created.[112] The solution is the recovery of glory, not in any self-centered or self-initiated effort, but solely in Jesus Christ. There is one glory: the glory of God. All others are counterfeit. To realize, to receive the one true glory, we must renounce any self-glory.

This is why all man-made codes must eventually fail. They are based on pride and informed by subjectivity. Call it humanism or any other human "-ism," it is the sin that Adam and Eve taught all their children. We would be our own gods; to define for ourselves what constitutes good and evil. If that means suddenly realizing our nakedness, we will sew our own loincloths, thank you. But fig leaves are a pitiful substitute for divine glory.[113]

In the previous chapter we set out the proposition of an absolute and ultimate truth as personified in Jesus Christ. This truth enlightens not only our theology or our metaphysic but also our ethics and morality. If we are to speak of ethical systems or moral codes at all, we must recognize a norm, a final criterion, an objective and constant standard of right and wrong. Otherwise, Calvin was correct in the last chapter; my way is just as good as yours and is no better than Hitler's.

We have to have that thermometer,[114] that objective indicator of reality that is absolute rather than relative. In my willful fallenness, I demand my autonomy. But while it galls me to say so, what I really *need* is Someone to tell me what to do. I haven't done so well just depending on my own wisdom.

And please, no more of that psychological sophistry that would label such confession a neurotic abdication of personal responsibility. Choose any period of my personal history or our species' history. Every one of them will prove the confession irrefutably true: I—we—need a Director!

---

111 Genesis 1:27.
112 Romans 3:23.
113 See Genesis 3.
114 See page 81.

Situation ethicists claim to have found the thermometer, the proper—even Christian—middle ground between Antinomianism and Pharisaism. They don't deny the existence of any absolutes but they do limit the number to a single one: love; ("justice-love" is the term currently in vogue). My task as a disciple, they say, is to determine for myself what love is to do in any given situation. I may refer to the Bible for examples of how love acted in other times and places. That may or may not be how love is to act at this time and place. Situationists rightly define love (*agapē*) as active good will, a product of godly volition rather than human emotion. And this love, they claim, is the only guideline I need.

I confess to a certain initial sympathy for this approach. I've seen the damage done by those who would reduce all of God's word to nothing more than a rigid checklist of simplistic do's and don'ts. They have God and his word in a box; they have a hard and fast rule for every contingency. They are right and they know they are right—even when they're dead wrong. There is a seductive kind of simple security in such a binary, yes-or-no religion but again and again, Jesus warned against such smug legalism. The genius of his entire Sermon on the Mount is a call to go deeper than the letter to the all encompassing spirit of the Law. In the Sermon, I find the applications broadening—and my loopholes closing—as I realize that, to God, my rage is homicidal and my lust is adulterous.[115]

I must admit that I have been confronted with very difficult situations for which simple black-and-white answers were not so readily available. Sometimes, God calls me to take his love into uncharted waters, trusting his grace, his truth and his Spirit. But even in my caution against simplistic, cookbook answers, I must beware of situationist arguments as well. Some are based almost entirely on exceptional events or hypothetical situations, such as the decision to drop a nuclear bomb on one country to stop a world war. Life is so seldom made of these situations that making their demands the norm is deceptive. We don't often have to scream, "Fire!" at our neighbor; screaming at our neighbor is not something to consider in our set of daily behavioral rules.

I must remember that Jesus did not say, "Love is my only command." He said, "If you love me, you will keep my commands."[116] While it is

---

115 Matthew 5-7.
116 John 14:15.

quite true that everything Jesus commanded is love in action, it does not follow that I can discard the specific commands and retain only the love. A command is more than a vague illustration or example of morality from which I am to draw analogies.

The situationist's definition of Christian love is correct—as far as it goes. But it is disastrously incomplete apart from the entire body of Jesus' instructions. They are nothing less than *divine* definitions of love. They tell me how love should act when I, in my weakness, subjectivity and limited perspective, cannot rightly make that determination.

Of course, I must resist the comfort I find in scripture-twisting legalism. But I must also admit that, left to me, my great ethical justice-love easily degenerates into a soft, shortsighted and self-serving trifle far removed from the massive, rugged love of Jesus. Even when my motives are the purest, my insights are still grievously deficient. So I will do well to remember that, as they say, God gave Moses the Ten Commandments, not the Ten Suggestions.

Called not to a system but to a self-denied/Christ-realized obedience, I then will be scrupulously honest with God's word, letting it be nothing more nor less than what it is. I will hear the direct commands in all their thrust and clarity. And I will hear the broad guidelines and moral principles in all their sweep and subtlety. I will note carefully the original context and intent, and I will embrace fully the lasting authority and relevance of God's living word, this razor-sharp and double-edged sword of the Spirit.[117]

In discussing this chapter with fellow writer, Jane Gibson (the perfume of whose artistry and intellect suffuses this book literally from cover to cover) I told her I was concerned with sounding self-contradictory in this section. Do I seem to side with the legalists against the situationists in one paragraph only to sound in the next paragraph like a situationist rebuffing the legalists? Jane graciously said that she understood what I was saying; then referring to the quotation of John 14:15 above, she said, "When Jesus says, 'If you love me,' he's making it personal. He isn't asking me to produce some vague imitation of him because I admire him and approve of his style. Instead, I *want* to obey him as a way to honor and adore him, to show how much I love him and want to please him." And it's true that when I truly

---

117 Hebrews 4:12.

fix my thoughts on Jesus,[118] I no longer think in terms of "commands" that must be obeyed versus "suggestions" that can be overlooked. As Jane put it, "The merest hint of what pleases him is what I want to do."

Picking up on my phrase "cookbook answers," Jane said, "With Christ, I'm a bride in love, learning to cook for my Groom. If I know of precise recipes he enjoys I follow them exactly. Over time, I learn his tastes and even when there's no recipe available to follow, I instinctively do what I know he likes. Sometimes the dish may not be what I like, but that's not important. I like pleasing Him. I don't just make dinner because it's my *job*; it becomes my *joy*, another way to show my love!"

I simply want to "find out what pleases the Lord."[119] So I search the Scriptures to learn the ways I can delight my Lord with my obedience. And when faced with a confusing moral dilemma, I remember that it is no longer I making all those decisions, but Christ living in me. What a relief! I *do* have the mind of Christ.[120] It becomes not merely second nature but my new true nature to do, purely and simply, what he wants me to do.

I don't have to speculate, "What would (the long ago and far away) Jesus do?" I can ask, "What is Jesus doing?" And then by the power of his Spirit I can do it! The more I ask (and seek and knock), the more natural, even reflexive this obedience becomes. He fills me more and more with himself. I grow to like what he likes and dislike what he dislikes. I learn to see the world as he sees it. I learn to do in this world what he did when he walked here, what he continues to do as he now walks here in his disciples. And so I find my love growing and overflowing with increasing knowledge, insight and ability to learn what is best.[121]

So what does that make me? A situational legalist? A legalistic situationist? Some of both? All I know is that my Lord makes me a Christian, and whether I embrace a lawless ethic, a code ethic or even a situation ethic, they all will fail me if I have set myself up as my own standard. I can't devise an exhaustive legal catalog to establish my own righteousness. Nor can I trust myself to be my own law or my heart to be its own standard of love.

---

118 Hebrews 3:1.
119 Ephesians 5:10.
120 I Corinthians 2:16.
121 Philippians 1:9, 10.

Only through self-denial/Christ-realization can I come to know the divine love that is empowered to do the divine will. Only through self-denial/Christ-realization do I discover the Good News that I don't have to go about this matter of ethics all alone.

A postscript: Much has been said of late about the rediscovery of virtue and values in our culture. Certainly, we take hope in this development but it is cautious hope. Social conservatives have been severely ridiculed for suggesting that a two-parent home is a better choice than a one-parent home—until it was understood that the benefit could be measured in dollars and cents. So we really decided that two parent homes are right? Or have we just come to realize that they are more socio-economically sound?

Aren't we reaffirming virtue primarily because it works? It is pragmatism, pure and simple. Virtue is an effective antidote for crime, welfare abuse and the spread of STD's. Well, of course, we should have known that all along. God knows best. His laws are not arbitrary burdens;[122] they are wonderfully efficient and beneficial. But as Christians, we embrace God's word simply because it is *from God*. He is sovereign. When he gives a command, ours is not to say, "Well, that certainly makes sense, so I'll do it." Ours is simply to trust and obey, when it makes sense to our finite minds and when it doesn't.

By self-denial/Christ-realization, we let God be God. And he grows us to be the persons we were designed to be. Our trust pleases him; our obedience acknowledges how much higher and holier are his ways.

The Love Generation and its progeny—left-wing and right-, traditional and revolutionary—have proven all too unlovely and unloving. But we are not unloved. There is a God in heaven who still would have us come and learn from him what love and truth really are. In Christ, we do not come before God's throne as criminals condemned by law or even slaves whose survival depends on their obedience to that law. We come as trusting children, joyful, thankful and assured that in the will of God we find our highest joy and truest delight.[123]

---

122 I John 5:3.
123 John 15:10, 11; Psalm 1:1, 2.

PART FIVE

The Faith
of
Christ

CHAPTER 11: "...BORN AGAIN"

Then change your thinking and turn around so that your sins may be wiped away, and that then times of refreshing may come from the Lord's presence as he sends the one already declared for you, the Anointed One, Jesus...

Acts 3:19, 20

Throughout my career, whether in church ministry or private practice, I've been involved in counseling. Some four decades of experience have made me appreciate just how rare change is. Oh, I know that inconsistency is the one consistency of human behavior. But what I'm talking about is substantive, core change. I've learned that when people say, "I've tried *everything*," they usually mean that they have tried every version of the *same* thing. And they aren't too impressed when I first suggest, "If what you're doing doesn't work, do something else." But sometimes they hang in there long enough to discover for themselves just how radical that little word "else" can be.

The Bible talks about the most radical *"something else"* of all, a change so thorough that it is described as new birth and as resurrection. It is the change called conversion.

Right here, you and I are up against a threefold problem:

1. We live in an age of linguistic inflation wherein words have been so overused and undervalued that they have lost their meaning.
2. We live in an age that tends to equate religious tolerance with spiritual indifference.

3. We live in an age of an insidious consumerism so pervasive that it has infected the church.

So for over thirty years now we have had all kinds of rebirths. We have "born again" golfers and joggers, "born again" Democrats and Republicans—you name it. *Now* what does "born again" mean anymore?

We pride ourselves on our slogans about freedom of religion. When first voiced, they may well have been thoughtful declarations about the personal responsibility of each individual to obey what he or she understands to be God's will. Today, the phrase tends to mean, "freedom *from* religion." Religious freedom from human dictates is not the same thing as religious autonomy that overrides divine dictates.

Nevertheless, in some quarters the gospel has been reduced to a commodity and converts have given way to consumers. "What's that? You don't have a taste for that god? Well, how about this one? It comes in five sizes, four colors ad three genders with a variety of optional laws, liturgies and lifestyles!"

So now that it's time to talk about conversion, it will be difficult for you and me to do so the way the apostles did. We tend to think of conversion as aligning ourselves with a given philosophy or ethic or church that generally reaffirms our preconceived notions. These days conversion can be a pleasant, proper, painless procedure far more akin to joining a club than to the radically upsetting process we read of in the book of Acts. As Gary Freeman opined,

> *The preacher pays a real compliment to his sermon when he concludes it by asking the audience to be converted. Significant changes of direction in anyone's life are rare...With a reasonably agile mind a man can accept religion, join a church, perform the necessary amenities, and never make any change more drastic, say, than giving up smoking. And most of the time he reneges on that.*[124]

Conversion in the Biblical sense is a turning around. More than swerving a few degrees this way or that, it is an about-face. As in Acts 3:19,

---

124 Gary Freeman, *Are You Going to Church More but Enjoying It Less?*, Austin, Texas: R. B. Sweet Company, 1967, p 34.

the Bible closely aligns the verbs *convert* and *repent*.[125] Both terms speak of thorough change. Biblical repentance is, literally, a change of mind. Again though, we must think of change in that absolute sense. I "change" my mind every day. That is, I make minor adjustments and modifications of little significance—whether to have dessert, what TV show to watch, or what shirt to wear. But almost never is my mind essentially, radically changed.

A few years ago near my birthday, Janet ran across a sign that said, "Great news! The lab called: Your brain is ready." When she bought it for me, little did she know that in just a few days the doctors would tell me that I had to have brain surgery. Fortunately, the operation wasn't nearly as radical as that accidental prophecy, but I still have that sign to remind me.

Beyond that physical gray matter, though, there is the *psyche*, the very soul itself. Of that essence, you might say that, while I have had many changes of mind, I have had only one change of minds. It was not a brain transplant but a gracious exchange of my carnal mind for the very mind of Christ.

Christian conversion is, in a word, revolutionary. That is precisely the word. But like "born again" or "unique" or "new" or a host of other words ravaged by Madison Avenue, "revolutionary" has become anemic. Imagine, if you can, that you've never heard the term used in reference to cake mixes or cosmetics.

Jesus is *the* Revolutionary of all time. And Christian conversion is revolutionary not only because of the degree of change it involves but because of the very nature of that change, a change of who and what a person will become. Merely *religious* conversion can involve nothing more than acceptance of a set of ideas. True *Christian* conversion requires surrender to a Person. More than the adoption of a given dogma or lifestyle, conversion is, first of all, to Jesus of Nazareth and then because of him, it is conversion to his ethic, his company and his mission.

I am not converted because, as a demonstration of kindness, I stop along life's road to pick up a hitch-hiker named Jesus. I am not converted

---

125 The Greek verb *epistepho*, rendered "turn around" in this chapter's opening scripture, is also translated "convert" or "be converted," "turn again," etc. The Greek verb *metanoew*, to change one's mind or purpose, is usually represented by the English, "repent."

because I've tucked a Bible in the glove box for emergencies. I am not converted because I have a cruciform hood ornament to show my piety or a bumper sticker that reveals my theological chic. I am converted when I turn over to Jesus the vehicle's title, registration and steering wheel, fully aware that his first maneuver may be a U-turn.

I cannot come to Jesus looking for endorsement of my basic goodness or enhancement of my self image. Conversion is denial of myself rather than adding Christ to myself. Conversion is death to self. At the deepest and truest level, conversion speaks to my most fundamental instincts and longings. But to my old self, conversion is just as radical and counter-instinctual as suicide. However, Bonhoeffer rightly objects to equating self-denial and suicide, "for there is an element of self-will even in that."[126] Rather than a suicide, conversion to Christ is that initial glad submission to execution.

This sounds like anything but good news until we remember that conversion is death only because it then can be rebirth. Conversion is resurrection into the Christlife. Out of the death to sin and self, God raises an altogether new person with the same life of power and eternity with which Jesus walked out of his tomb. The righteousness of Christ has been imputed and his Spirit imparted. The new person has turned again to walk not only in a new direction but within a new *dimension*.

Conversion, then, is nothing less than that first response to the command to deny self, take up the cross and follow Jesus. It is the believer's introduction to his life's new dynamic, self-denial/Christ-realization.

Scripture speaks often of this transformation. I have two favorite passages. The first is the stunning third chapter of John where Jesus himself first reveals the need for being born again. Here Nicodemus, a leader of the Pharisee, comes to our Lord in the night, confessing that Jesus is a rabbi from God. Jesus responds by declaring that one must be born again[127] in order to see the kingdom of God.

---

126 Bonhoeffer, p. 97.

127 *Gennethei anothen*, "born again," might also be rendered, "born from above." *Anothen*, somewhat like our word "over," refers to something upward or, more precisely, from above. But it also can carry the meaning, "from the first," or "from before" more or less like "over" in the phrase, "over again." Given John's consistent use of *anothen* elsewhere as "from above" (3:31; 19:11, 23) and his descriptions of birth always in terms of origin (of God, of flesh, of the Spirit, of water), "born from (of) above" may be a better translation. It's not unlikely that John intended both meanings.

When Nicodemus protests that an adult cannot re-enter the mother's womb to be born anew, Jesus replies,

> *In all truth I tell you, unless born of water and Spirit, one cannot enter God's kingdom.*

Here is a declaration of a mystery so profound that even the expert Nicodemus doesn't get it at first. He is familiar enough with the opening words of Genesis where the Spirit of creation is portrayed as hovering over the waters. He, no doubt, has heard about John the Baptist immersing people in Jordan's waters to signify their repentance—their change of mindset. Nicodemus might even have heard of the Baptist's prophecy of one who would baptize with the Holy Spirit,[128] the Spirit of the *new* creation. But how does all this tie into that peculiar phrase, "born again?" Unlike us, Nicodemus has never heard it before. It's shocking. It's impossible. A whole new birth? From above?

We are never told how or when Nicodemus comes to appreciate all that Jesus was saying. We do see him later assisting Joseph of Arimathea in preparing Jesus' body for the tomb.[129] I wonder if any thoughts of resurrection accompany his attention to this death and burial. I wonder if he has any idea how his actions this day relate back to his questions that night when Jesus talked not of death but birth.

Such pondering leads me to the book of Romans and my other favorite description of the nature, the meaning and the implications of our conversion experience. Paul taught salvation by grace through faith apart from works of the law. His critics claimed that, taken to its logical end, Paul's gospel would have us sinning all the more so that there could be an even greater abundance of God's grace. In Romans 6:1-14, he gave the definitive response to that accusation. He insisted that we cannot *live* in sin because we have *died* to sin. Our old self was executed in union with the crucified Christ who died to sin once for all. So now our old body of sin is dead and powerless. In union with the resurrection of Christ, the new self is alive, not to sin, but strictly to God.

Paul puts it in a fascinating way in 6:3, 4. In order to allow the full impact of Paul's imagery, we will use "immersed" in place of "baptized."

---

128 See John 1:19-34.
129 John 19:39.

While various definitions of baptism may be debated today, Paul's original audience would have recognized simply that he was talking about a dipping, a dunking, a submerging, a "burial" in water (and in Spirit).

> *Or don't you know that all of us who were immersed into Christ Jesus were immersed into his death? Therefore, through this immersion, we were buried with him into that death so that just as Christ was raised from the dead through the glory of the Father, so we also might walk in newness of life!*

Is it possible for you and me to hear those words in the same way the Romans first did? We bring nearly two thousand years worth of baggage to this passage, don't we? Baptism has always involved mystery; for the modern western mind that mystery is compounded. Why baptism? What's the big deal? Then there are all those debates, not just about immersion versus sprinkling or pouring, but about the very purpose and significance of baptism. What does it have to do with the new birth, the birth from above?

Listening to some of the debates, you would think that there are only two possible—and mutually exclusive—answers to those questions. One seems to treat baptism as an arbitrary but effective sacrament that, in and of itself, saves its beneficiary. At the opposite end of the spectrum, there seems to be an idea that baptism is a rather unimportant, elective sort of follow-up to conversion. So some talk only of a sacrament while others talk merely of an after-the-fact symbol, both insisting that there is no third alternative.

The first group certainly can make a case from scripture. I've often heard...

"Acts 2:38 shows that, from the very beginning, the apostles called on people to repent and be baptized for the forgiveness of sins. In Acts 22:16, even after Saul (Paul) had a miraculous confrontation with Christ, Ananias still instructed him to 'be baptized and wash away your sins.' Later, Paul wrote not only Romans 6 but Colossians 2:12 which also says that in baptism we were buried and raised with Christ. In Galatians 3:27, he says that it was in baptism that we were united with and even clothed with Christ. Why, I Peter 3:21 even says that baptism now saves us...."

From the other side of the aisle comes: "You're quoting all those passages out of context. The whole point of Paul's letters to the Romans and the Galatians is that we are saved by grace through faith apart from works. Just read the three chapters that precede Romans 6, or everything in Galatians that leads up to 3:27. Then there's Ephesians 2:8-9 and other passages that say exactly the same thing. As for I Peter 3:21, it goes on to say that the important thing is the answer of a good conscience toward God. Romans 10:9 summarizes it all quite clearly and simply when it says to believe in your heart and you will be saved..."

"Speaking of quotes out of context!"

Let's get away from a proof-text-fest and take the path of self-denial/Christ-realization. It's been leading us in the right direction all along and there's every reason to believe it will do so in this matter, too. I'm not about to argue against a single one of God's words cited above, all the way from Acts 2:38 to Romans 10:9. But I will argue that they all are best understood in light of those two great self-denial/Christ-realization passages, Matthew 16:24 and Galatians 2:20.

What better enacts self-denial/Christ-realization than an experience in which we die, are buried, and then are resurrected? What a grand inauguration ceremony God, in his wisdom, has given us! A symbol? Absolutely, but not merely a symbol.[130] As M. R. Vincent put it over a century ago, "...the rite, through its association with the Spirit's energy...is a veritable vehicle of grace to the recipient, and acquires a substantial part in the inauguration of the new life."[131]

The New Testament picture of baptism consistently involves candidates who, accountable and cognizant, enter the water in total submission to God's sovereignty and full acceptance of God's grace. It is not a work they do to earn salvation; it is not some magical mechanism through which they obligate God or manipulate grace. They simply surrender the crucified self to God who buries the old person and raises the new creature. In

---

130 Biblical writers, ancient and eastern, probably viewed symbols and their subjects as much more intimately connected than we modern westerners do. So whether we are talking about baptism, the Lord's supper, or whatever, we may do ourselves and the text a great disservice when, in our thinking, we reduce Biblical symbols to mere tokens or illustrations.

131 M. R. Vincent, *Word Studies in the New Testament,* Wilmington, Delaware: Associated Publishers and Authors, 1972, p. 414.

submitting to this burial, the recipients have not merited redemption; they have, instead, trusted their Savior to meet them in this divinely appointed trysting place. By a wonder of God's grace they have become engaged, involved, immersed in the great redemptive event, the death, burial and resurrection of Christ.

No wonder Beasley-Murray calls baptism a *drastic* experience. In *Baptism in the New Testament,* one of the Twentieth Century's most outstanding works on the subject, he writes of baptism as "supremely the occasion when God draws near in Christ to a man drawing near to Him in faith."[132]

He goes on then to talk of the fundamentally passive nature of baptism. In essence, our baptism is not a work which we ourselves can perform. Notwithstanding the hypothetical fellow who has to immerse himself because he's stranded on an island, the essential nature of baptism and that which it enacts is passive. I cannot crucify myself. I may commit suicide in any number of ways but not by nailing both my hands to a cross! And once I am dead, I cannot bury my own corpse. Nor can I, by any means, effect my own resurrection.

So it is with my conversion. I do willingly submit; I do penitently deny self and confess Christ. But the realization of the Christlife, the appropriation of his righteousness is not my doing. True Christian baptism has never been a human work. It is God's work. It is God's gift. He crucifies me; he buries me; he raises me up. Human agency is so emphatically irrelevant that Paul even chastised the Corinthians for attaching any significance to the identity of the person who dunked them in the water.[133] Rather, in concert with other New Testament writers, he consistently emphasized the Person—the Holy Spirit—who immersed them into Christ.

Someone once shared with me a comparison of the conversion process with that of human reproduction. He spoke of the impregnation with the word, then the gestation of this embryonic new life through repentance and the first confession of faith, and finally the birth of the new creature coming up out of the baptismal waters. And it is God, the Parent, not the helpless infant, who produces that new life.

---

132 G. R. Beasley-Murray, *Baptism in the New Testament,* Grand Rapids: William B. Eerdmans Publishing Company, 1972, p. 132.
133 I Corinthians 1:12-17.

What could be more consistent with the grace/faith nature of our salvation? Our debaters both were saying some true and important things. All they needed to balance their perspectives was the right starting point, and that is self-denial/Christ-realization. Our faith, and thus our baptism into that faith, is not about *us* at all. It is *all* about Christ! As with the previous chapter's legalist and libertine who both ended up in the same camp of selfism, both our debaters are starting with the self, in this case, the baptismal *candidate*. Thus they both keep missing the point (and are both partly right in saying that the other is wrong). But if they start with Christ, the true baptismal *Agent*, they will surely see how the same Paul could write Romans 4 as well as Romans 6.

Our gracious Father knows just how very subjective and inconsistent we are. He has anticipated our dark hours of doubt when the questions come: Am I really saved? What if I wasn't penitent enough? What if I didn't pray hard enough to get all the way through? How do I know that I really am a Christian?

Then there are the questions of young people reared in Christian homes: Where is the radical transformation I was told to expect? Why don't I feel like I'm going in a whole new direction? Why haven't I too felt something "drastic?"

May we turn once more to Beasley-Murray? His continued exposition of Romans 6 has something crucial to say about all these questions.

> *Baptism, and the Christian faith it embodies, is rooted in the 'Christ event', with all that it implies, and nothing of man's doing and no theological explanation must ever be allowed to detract from the uniqueness, splendour and power of that event. To be united with Christ in his redemptive acts, and therefore to enter into His death and resurrection, cannot but have catastrophic consequences for the believer. His old life is set under the judgment of the cross and a new man begins to live. No less language than death and resurrection can suffice to describe the nature of the transition from the old creation to the new. That the experience is bound up with such an overt act as baptism serves to make it the more objective, the more definite, the more tangible.[134]*

---

134 Beasley-Murray, 138.

God consummates my conversion experience in baptism. Is this a bit too arbitrary or concrete on God's part? Of course not; it is perfect. My new birth has an objective, time-space reference point.[135] I don't have to decide which prayer was the one. I don't need to monitor my emotions to decide precisely when felt desire becomes felt fulfillment. Yes, I am called of God to walk—to continue—in a new life which bears fruit. But I don't have to wait for the fruit to appear before I can be sure of my salvation. God has given me a definite and tangible place to drive the peg. Then and there, he washed me in the blood saving me by grace through faith. And nothing—no feeling, no doubt, no trial, no failure, no accusation—can change that fact. Praise God!

But what if my rebirth didn't *feel* quite that "drastic" or "catastrophic?" In that case, my baptism reminds me that rebirth is a matter of God's objective promise, not my subjective emotions. Even if I was brought up in a thoroughly Christian home, even if Jesus has always been my best Friend, accepting him as my only Savior needn't be a routine or anticlimactic event.

Earlier in the chapter we spoke of conversion as a change not only of direction but dimension. Even if I was brought up always to walk in that right direction, my conversion experience will be no less drastic a change of dimension. I still love Jesus and his word. I still seek to do his will. But now there is an important difference, one that *is* there when I feel it and when I don't. Now it is no longer I but Christ living in me! I am born again. I am cleansed of all sin. I have begun a whole new life, the eternal life. There absolutely *has* been a catastrophic change, if not so much in life style, certainly in life dynamic. For now it isn't just me working out my salvation but God at work in me providing the will and the ability.[136]

And when clouds of doubt block the sun of reality, I can still rejoice. For the authenticity and effectiveness of my conversion depend neither on the depth of my understanding nor the height of my emotion. Rather, they

---

135 While a linear or sequential perspective on the conversion process is useful and appropriate, that usefulness is limited. Too many arguments have centered on sequence with attempts at pinpointing the precise moment of redemption. Another approach, at least as useful but with which our western minds are less comfortable, is a *gestalt* or unified view of the conversion experience. This sees the process as a seamless whole and makes no attempt to segment it or rank its various components. Everything in this chapter is written in sympathy with this latter view, even when the language is necessarily linear.

136 Philippians 2:12, 13.

are anchored firmly in the saving work done once for all in Jesus Christ who by grace has consented to share his life with, of all people, me!

So there is now no condemnation for those in Christ Jesus!
Romans 8:1

CHAPTER 12: "...SEATED...IN THE HEAVENLIES..."

Our Father in the heavens,
Hallowed, your Name,
Come, your reign,
Done, your will,
As in heaven, so on earth.
Matthew 6:9, 10

Do you have an ear for music? How would you describe that grating vibration created by the sound of two tones just one fourth to one half step apart?

Or do you have an eye for color? I thought I did until the day I almost got out of the house wearing a pair of olive pants with a sea-green shirt. You should have heard Janet shriek! And shriek again when I said, "But they're both green..." In my defense, I must say that Janet had still been asleep when I was first dressing, so there was very little light in the room.

Or do you have a palate for fine flavor combinations? How about fresh, tart grapefruit washed down with sweet, whole milk?

Dissonant, clashing incompatibility—disharmony, misalliance, incongruity. Sometimes it seems to affect every facet of existence, making life a paralyzing puzzle. This isn't a problem of only modern living; consider these word from two millennia ago:

In practice, what happens? My own behavior baffles me. For
I find myself not doing what I really want to do but doing
what I really loathe.

Romans 7:15 (Phillips)

Acts. 2:36
17:

122

The amazing thing about Romans 7 is that it sits there right next to Chapter 8. In one chapter you have Paul calling himself a wretched bundle of self-contradiction, crying out to be rescued. Then he starts the next chapter with that remarkable verse about no condemnation—present tense! He goes on to talk about life in the Spirit who is at work in our daily lives, in our prayers, in *all* things so that nothing is able to separate us from divine love! Where is the congruity in these two chapters?

Congruity. How many times have you experienced congruity? You know: those times when everything really does work together. Everything is in tune, in synch, in agreement. All parts are consistent with and appropriate to each other, with no contradiction. It all fits. It all makes sense. In place of dissonance, there is resonance; in place of discord, concord. Where there was a kind of disintegration, now there is a single integrity. It all sounds right, looks right and tastes right. You really have your act *together*.

This must be what it was like constantly in the Garden before the fall. That has to be what it is like eternally in the new Paradise. But what about right here, right now? Now—when *there is no condemnation*? And now—when *I don't even know what I'm doing*?

In his letter to the Ephesians, Paul says something quite remarkable about you and me. He begins by saying that God has blessed us with every spiritual blessing *in the heavenlies in Christ*.[137] After listing some of those blessings, he speaks of his prayers on behalf of Christians. One of his petitions is that they will know the very power by which God *raised Christ from the dead and seated him at his right hand in the heavenlies*.[138] After three more verses on the exalted Christ, Paul begins to talk of *our* resurrection. Though we were dead in our sins, he brought us to life in Christ by grace. With and in Christ, God literally *co-quickened* us, *co-resurrected* us and yes, *co-seated us in the heavenlies in Christ Jesus!*[139] You and I "have died and gone to heaven!" Really! Let it sink in. By the resurrecting power of God, by the unbounded grace of God and in the eternal, glorified Christ who

---

137 Ephesians 1:13.
138 Ephesians 1:20.
139 Ephesians 2:5, 6.

now *is far above all other rule and authority and power and dominion,*[140] you have been placed in heaven. Past tense, present reality!

Why do I feel quick to add that this is only a representative reality, as if that somehow moderates or diminishes it? It is still the greater reality, the eternal reality. Its representative nature only increases its greatness because of *who* my Representative is. Cloaked in the very splendor of Christ, so glorious that it renders all my blemishes invisible, I have now been ushered into the divine Presence. Apart from Christ, that Presence could have been only my undoing. In Christ, it is my perfecting.

But how do I bring all that down to earth where I still see the blemishes in the mirror and the mundane all around me? How do I find congruity?

The Model Prayer, quoted in part at the opening of this chapter, begins with three great interlinking petitions. The translation tries to capture the impact of the original in which the verb emphatically introduces each request—*hallowed, come, done*—poetically stressing their urgency. We might paraphrase,

> *Our Abba*[141] *in the highest majesty:*
> *Our greatest desire is*
> *the **honoring** of your very being,*
> *the **advancing** of your kingdom reign,*
> *and the **completing** of your will,*
> *as your final, perfect reality*
> *floods over into our existence even here, even now!*

In my private prayer life, I have come to personalize that last phrase, *as in heaven, so on earth,* combining it in my mind with Ephesians 2:6. I think in terms of my "heaven-self" and my "earth-self." The phrase thus becomes a prayer for congruity, not only on a cosmic scale but also in very personal, practical sense. "Let that grace-bestowed, final, perfect self

---

140 Ephesians 1:21.

141 This Aramaic term is the word Jesus used to address the Father in the Gethsemane prayer (Mark 14:36) and, arguably, every place where the Greek text shows Jesus addressing God as *patér* ("father"). "Father" is an accurate translation but *abba* may connote the greater intimacy of terms like "papa" or "daddy" yet without any of the irreverence suggested by various colloquial uses of these words. So it becomes almost untranslatable; indeed, both Mark and Paul (Romans 8:15; Galatians 4:6) elect to use the untranslated term itself. *Abba* uniquely underscores the profound intimacy Christ shares with the Father, an intimacy that, by the power of the indwelling Spirit of Christ, we share.

in heaven flood over into the here-and-now existence of self on earth. I want earth-self to be one with heaven-self in unambiguous, unadulterated, undistracted accord. Oh Father, resolve the dissonance!"

The false resolutions, the counterfeit congruities are too easy, too tempting, too infernal. Perhaps the most common is to give in to the earth-self as if it is the only reality. Sometimes my task just seems too formidable. If I can't be what I really want then maybe I can convince myself to want what I apparently am. Sure, it's an admission of defeat but at least when my head hits the pillow tonight that dissonance won't be ringing in my ear. It will be just one note—not the most beautiful in tone, but unison at least.

But when night does come, what I hear is not the clear simple tone of my own single note but a hellish cacophony infinitely worse than the dissonance I fled. Before, at least one instrument was in tune. Now none is.

Perhaps, then, I can settle for a shallow, simplistic faith that acts as if God can be tamed and put on a leash. Earth-self will win heaven-self over with pat answers and infantile piety. Like the bellowing church tenor who has no idea how flat he is, I'll merrily keep screeching my naive little ditty, comfortable in my assumption that I am right in tune with heaven.

But it can be only assumption, for I am not listening to heaven so much as I am expecting heaven to listen to me. Anyway, my ears keep getting this waxy build-up of simple-minded self-righteousness.

I think some of the mid-life crises I have observed may be a combination of these two false resolutions. Start with a lifetime of comfortable, simplistic religion and morality. On the surface, it may even look like a robust devotion. But not very far under that surface is an approval-motivated and self-centered religiosity that has never squarely faced the tough questions. In fact, it may have been so busy removing specks from the eyes of others that it has become blind to the piece of lumber gouging its own eye.[142]

Then one day the mirror talks back, "Your life is half over and where has all your churchy behavior gotten you? Your kids are getting more distant by the day. Your mate is hardly thrilled with you any more. You were passed up for Young Citizen of the Year a decade ago and you may never make it to the Senior Citizen competition. Get real for once in

---

142 Matthew 7:3.

your life! Drop the Goody-Two-Shoes facade, resign as Sunday School teacher, take the retirement money, buy the sports car and run off with that graduate teenager."

Right here, we need to make a clear distinction between simplism and simplicity. The resonance of heaven and earth that we seek is not simple-minded but it is simple. It is what the Bible calls "singleness."[143] The word represents noble simplicity, a oneness or singularity that is free from inner discord, ulterior motives or ambiguity. It carries the ideas of purity, wholeness and wholeheartedness; a singleness of heart, mind and purpose. Just a few verses after Matthew records the model prayer, he gives us these words of the Master:

> *The lamp of the body is the eye: so if your eye is single [pure, good, clear, free from blurred or double vision], your whole body will be bathed in light.* Matthew 6:22

Single Vision: Christ and Him Crucified
Christ is all in all.

That's what I want. I'm tired of seeing double. God, give me focus; give me that singleness of sight even while all these earth-scenes flood my vision! One Lord One Faith One Baptism

How?

How does he do it? First by helping me understand that I don't do it. that I can't do it. Whatever follows in the remaining pages of this book, I beg you not read it as an instruction manual on how *we* accomplish congruity. Rather, I pray it can serve as a trembling introduction to how *God* can achieve, and we can receive, that oneness.

He begins by unveiling for me the beauty and truth in the paradox of losing my life to find it. I lose myself to find my true self, the heaven-self that Christ sees, the new self that Christ creates. Gradually, he clarifies for me this authentic sense of identity, this growing awareness of who and whose I really am. He honors my petition for the kingdom come as heaven descends to earth and the King makes my heart his domain. He enables me to "get real" indeed, for this is the true me! This is the eternal me. And the

---

143 *Haplotes* (In Romans 12:8; II Corinthians 8:2, 9:11, and 9:13 it is rendered "liberality" or "generosity." In II Corinthians 11:3; Ephesians 6:5; Colossians 3:22, the rendering is "simplicity" or "sincerity.") and the adjective *haplous*, "single" (Matthew 6:22; Luke 11:34).

only way I know to acknowledge or accept heaven-self is to acknowledge and accept heaven's Man, Jesus Christ.

Daily, I deny self and realize Christ. Daily, I turn from the mirror and to the Cross. But there also I see a reflection, no longer earthly but heavenly. And I can believe it because it is *his* truth, certified by his blood! That surety doesn't depend on me at all, not even on my consistency in maintaining the feeling or withstanding the doubt. It is his reality, so it remains firm even when I don't.

I am so accustomed to seeing the temporal—the temporary—as somehow more real, more substantial. The spiritual—the truly substantial—seems rather pale, ghostly and insubstantial—exceedingly difficult to keep in focus. Perhaps Jesus continually taught in parables to train us to see the heavenly beyond the earthly, to grasp the significance, the *significance.*

Just as he empowers me to see his body beyond the bread and his blood beyond the wine, he empowers me to see what surrender really is. Where once I thought it was an earthly self striving to attain the heavenly, he now reveals a heavenly self taking captive the earthly. Clearly this is not my doing; for me alone it would be simply impossible. Paul collides with this impossibility, and he cries out, "Wretched man that I am, who will rescue me from this body of death? Well, thanks be to God—through Jesus Christ our Lord!" Romans 7:24, 25a.

This "body of death" becomes a holy temple of the divine. It still moves through a temporal and temporary world but now that world is a planet of parables that teach me of the spiritual and the eternal. My whole life becomes still another of Christ's parable-songs.[144] And as I grow accustomed to the light, focus becomes sharper, and perception shifts. What I thought was substance is shadow; what I thought were filmy ghosts are *real* angels.

In the previous chapter we spoke of conversion as a union with the death and resurrection of Christ. But the story doesn't end with the empty tomb; it goes on to the Christ's ascension into heaven. Now Ephesians 2:6 says, in effect, "Just as your baptism bore witness to the death, burial

Infant – whatever I feel like doing
Child   Approval Level
Adult   make decisions about right and wrong
Alignment with Christ

---

144 In the portion of Ephesians that we have been considering, there is another marvelous statement. In 2:10, Paul says that we are God's workmanship. The word is *poiema* from which we get the English word poem. One is tempted to translate, "God's masterpiece."

and resurrection of your Lord, now your life is to be a testimony to his ascension."

"Take up your cross daily." What if I would wake each and every morning only to die, and die only to rise, and rise only to ascend so that God could then use me as a Jacob's ladder with which to bring some heaven-reality to this earth? A conduit through which the risen and glorified Christ could continue his redemptive ministry? Even as I write these words, my fingers weaken and my eyes sting. I feel as if I am dancing on the edge of the most presumptuous blasphemy. And, in fact, I am. Unless. Unless by grace, it really is no longer I but Christ.

I don't fully understand it. I don't readily feel it. I don't consistently show it. But by grace I believe it: In Christ I have died and gone to heaven. I believe, Lord. Help my unbelief![145]

> *Lord, lift me up and let me stand*
> *By faith on heaven's table land,*
> *A higher plane than I have found,*
> *Lord plant my feet on higher ground.*[146]

Having taught me to acknowledge the reality, now God can free me to celebrate the simplicity. Heaven-self can sing the melody and teach earth-self the harmony of simplicity's song. They can sing even in the midst of earth's confusion, contradiction and complexity; for this song is simple, not shallow.

I can become more attuned to expecting, seeking, discovering and celebrating all that is simple, real, pure. I can make a point of recognizing it whenever and wherever it occurs—in myself, in others I meet, in every aspect of God's creation. Do you suppose that is what Paul was getting at when he told Titus that to the pure, all things are pure?[147] To the single-minded, everything goes back to that one simple reality. And lifestyle is love's song in action, the servant life that greets each day with the simple refrain, "How can I be of help?" Now no task is too menial, no trial too overwhelming for they both are sanctified; both have been put to heaven's music.

---

145 Mark 9:24.
146 Johnson Oatman, Jr., *Higher Ground.*
147 Titus 1:15.

Suddenly, in fact, I gain a whole new perspective on God's commands. All those do's and don'ts once felt like the disrupters and complicators of my life—arbitrary tests and fun-spoilers. But now I can begin to realize what they really are. They are simplifiers, congruity tools—God's tuning forks that resolve my dissonance into harmony.

Jesus said that all the commands are variations on the one grand melody of love, love first for God and then for others.[148] Allow me a broad paraphrase of I John 3:18-24, using this congruity/harmony language:

> *Dear children, it's time to go beyond the words, "I love you," to the deeds. Make it actively, congruently real. Then that authentic harmony will resonate all the way down into your heart. You will know that you are in tune with the very presence of God even when you don't feel it—even when all you can hear is that old dirge of self-condemnation. You could never be a greater or more knowledgeable judge than God; yet, he has chosen not to condemn but to teach you how to transform that dirge into an anthem of assurance and victory. Then everything starts to harmonize: God provides what you ask, you do what he expects. And what does he expect? Faith. Faith in none other than his Son Jesus Christ. And loving behavior that is consistent with that faith, in tune with his song. Thus God creates a congruity so complete that we actually stay in him and he stays in us! His own Spirit indwelling us is our guarantee of that.*

God calls me—and empowers me—to practice congruity. In effect, he says, "You *are* it so *do* it. You don't have to wait until you feel perfectly consistent or capable. Just get started in the confidence that I, your Father, am perfectly consistent and capable. You are—right now—spiritual, heavenly, in Christ. Respond to that reality."

In Chapter Four we talked about three levels of behavior, the infant Feeling level, the child Approval level, and the adult Conscience level. Put in these terms, the practice of congruity begins by letting the *Christ-Centered Conscience* be the controlling level. Then, while reaching out in love to all people, I make sure to surround myself especially with God's people who *approve* and reinforce godly behaviors. No wonder Jesus (followed by Paul,

---

148 Matthew 22:37-40.

James and others) makes fellowship such a priority. Next, I repeat those behaviors enough to become accustomed to them. In time, I actually begin to *feel* most like my (new) self only when I am doing them. I allow God to order my life in such a way that it moves toward ever greater congruity at all levels. Whenever I find my self at odds with myself, the heaven-self must prevail. Whenever I am discordant, it may seem momentarily easier to flatten all the strings to the lowest one, but God gives me the Spirit and the grace to retune all the strings to the highest.

James speaks of the opposite of this singular reality. He talks about "double-minded" or "two-souled" people. They are the ones who second guess all their prayers, nullifying them with doubt (1:6-8). James also uses the term in reference to those whose pride would have them straddle the fence between God and the world (4:4-10). There he writes out a prescription for this kind of schizophrenia. The name of the medicine is Humble Submission. It contains a resisting agent and an approaching agent, a washing ingredient and a purifying ingredient. Here's how the combined formula acts:

1. *Resist the devil and he will flee from you.*

   That flight may take place sooner or much later but it *will* take place.

2. *Approach God and he will approach you.*

   That approach and its effectiveness are certain and stable; however, levels of subjective perception may vary.

   Note: This *Resist-Flee/Approach-Approach* combination is quite powerful and habit-forming.

3 & 4. *Wash your hands* and *Purify you hearts.*

   Another powerful combination, the cleansing is not only outward but inward. By the blood of Christ, the heart cleansing of the heaven-self is accompanied by the hand-cleansing of the earth-self.

   Take only as directed. Do not discontinue use.

But how about those doubts? Does James 1:8 say that I cannot pray again until I have managed to eradicate every feeling of doubt? If so, my prayer life just came to an end. Isn't it saying, rather, that as I pray, my trust can embrace my doubt, absorbing it and surrendering it as part of that faith-full prayer? So when I pray, as so often I must, "I believe, help my unbelief," even that apparent contradiction is part of the greater congruity. Faith means that I trust God even when I don't feel very trusting. It means acting as if I feel it because I know—I accept, I bet my very soul—that God is greater and truer than my feelings.

The resonance/harmony/congruity does not depend on my ability to develop and sustain a sense of perfect pitch but upon the absolute assurance that Christ always *is* the perfect pitch. He can use even my contrariness to drive me back to his constancy, my weakness to draw me to his strength, my helplessness to bring me to his succor. His grace is so great that he transforms even my incongruity into a subtext of his congruity. He absorbs my song of lamentation into his carol of redemption.

He is fully able to do this because he has been here; he knows all my struggles first hand. To come to him as I am is no affront to his holiness; rather, to turn away in my shame is the great insult to his incarnation.

So I look once more at Romans 7:24-8:1, recalling that Paul, "the wretch," cries out for rescue from his self-contradiction. Then immediately he thanks God who through Christ responds to that cry. Paul sets the stage for the eighth chapter which begins with the declaration of "no condemnation." But between the thanks of 7:25a and the declaration of 8:1, there are the peculiarly placed words of 7:25b:

> *So then , on the one hand, I serve the law of God with my mind, but on the other hand, I serve the law of sin with my flesh.*

Why in the world did Paul wedge this restatement of the *problem* between the thanksgiving and declaration of the *solution*? Surely this verse is misplaced; I want it to go before 7:24.

Could it be that Paul is reminding me that God's consistency and congruity are effective even when mine are not? The solution, for now, is a process and, for the time being, part of that process is the struggle. But I still can say the thanks to God because even now his congruity can engulf my incongruity until that Day when perfecting becomes perfection.

Finally, God calls me to a life—a ministry—of oneness. I am to look for simple unity everywhere I go. I am to work for it everywhere I am. I am to pray for it. I am to be it—a proclaimer, a celebrant, an exemplar. A creator, a reflection of unity, of wholeness, of the very oneness of God. In so doing, I become a singer in the choir of the cosmos. I take my seat in the heavenlies and, like the awestruck astronauts getting their first heaven's eye view of a single undivided earth, I scan the musical score God has placed before me. So many notes, so many parts, but one song!

I have yet to hear the entire ensemble; I simply perform my part though alone it may not always make musical sense to me. It may not be the melody or any of the notes I might have chosen. At times I might be tempted to take your line or even insist that you duplicate only mine. But by faith I can simply sing my part in the confidence that this is God's glory song, Christ's story song, and by sheer grace my song, my own *true* self song.

So we end this part of our discussion where it began, in those majestic opening chapters of Ephesians. The theme of that letter is the reunification of God's creation. Sin has dis-integrated the cosmos. In Christ, God is achieving the great re-integration of it all. Paul says in 1:9-10 that this is nothing less than the mystery of the universe. This is the Alpha and the Omega, the final cadence where God's grand composition reaches its ultimate resolution down to which song and story and celestial glories all come. This is the first word, the last word, the Word become flesh. In the dark night of the universe, this is the Star of Bethlehem. This is the Song of angels, *Gloria in excelsis deo.*[149] This is the Song of my heart, *Peace on earth.* In my inmost being, in all my relationships, in all the universe, *Christ is all and in all!*[150]

Reunion. Reconciliation. Harmony. Congruity.

ONE!

Let Go♡Let God

---

149 The Latin translation of Luke 2:14a, "Gory to God in the highest." The second half of the couplet says, "And on earth peace to those he favors."

150 Colossians 3:11.

CHAPTER 13: "...YOUR WILL BE DONE"

> *So let yourselves be humbled under the mighty hand of God, so that in time, he elevate you as you unload all your anxieties on him. Because to him, you matter.*
>
> *I Peter 5:6, 7*

What do you do when you feel absolutely overwhelmed? I'm not talking about a hard day at the office. I'm talking about an emotional heaviness that crushes your chest until you feel as if your lungs are going to collapse and your heart is going to burst. What do you do when every cell of your body is saturated with profound dread? Every fiber of your being tells you that you are doomed not only to die but first to suffer unspeakable agony. What do you do when those nearest and dearest to you seem a million miles away because there is no way they can comprehend the depth of your distress? You reach out to them, they reach out to you; but neither of you can span the gulf. What do you do when your nervous system is so stressed that your hands are ashen and aching for lack of blood? But the capillaries in your temples are so engorged and the pores so dilated that your sweat is not only profuse, it's actually bloody.

During my years of private practice, an area in which I specialized was panic and anxiety disorders. I have seen men and women hysterical with acute fear. I've recorded resting pulses in excess of 170 beats per minute. I've watched carotid arteries bulging and pulsating so wildly that I thought they might burst. But I have never seen or had a client report an episode of hemathidrosis. Most physicians will go through their entire careers without seeing a single case of that bloody perspiration. On the rarest of occasions, it has been reported in fox holes and gas chambers.

matt. 16:24
Follow His Command
Take up Cross & follow me

133

He is Able!

L. E. Hall

And a physician long ago reported an apparent case of hemathidrosis that occurred one evening in, of all places, a serene garden:

> *An angel from heaven appeared to him and strengthened him. Even so, his agony grew and his praying intensified as his sweat became like great blood-drops falling to the ground.*
>
> Luke 22:43, 44

So what do you do, on such a night, Lord?

I pray.

What do you pray, Lord?

I pray relief. I pray release. And then I pray, "Yet, not my will but yours."

Self-denial/Christ-realization, congruity, the power of One—it all comes down to this, the perfect prayer. "Your will be done", the most powerful, liberating, and unnatural prayer in human experience. The most natural and common prayer—with its innumerable disguises—is "my will be done." To be sure, I must bring my will—my desires and fears—to the Father. Even Jesus began the Gethsemane prayer with, *Let this cup pass from me.* So I, too, can bring my uncensored, innermost thoughts to God, but to bring them is to submit them. I bring them only to surrender them. Otherwise, I am not praying, I am negotiating—not with the sovereign God but a docile demigod.

Every disciple lives within the tension between heaven and earth, between *I believe* and *help my unbelief,* between *let this cup pass* and *yet not my will,* between *what physical life I do live now* and *I live in faith of the Son of God.* Daily we hear ourselves saying, *Today or tomorrow, we will go and we will do,* only to be reminded that we are *vapor.* So we correct our presumption by adding, *If the Lord wills.*[151]

When I first wrote the following paragraphs, I was describing my day. The material was dated even before the book was published. But even though that day is now over, I have again chosen to leave it as I first wrote it.

As I write these words, it is 4:00 PM, Tuesday, May 23, 1995. Exactly eight hours ago in Oklahoma City, the demolition crew razed what remained

---

151 James 4:13-16.

Imortal Horror or Everlasting Splendor which are you?

134

Care about the Kingdom and Righteousness and let worry take care of itself. Matt. 6: Don't Worry. No Longer I but Christ in me.

No Longer I

of the Alfred P. Murrah Federal Building. How could any of us ever forget April 19 and the worst act of terrorism in U. S. history? But there have been numberless other tragedies and catastrophes in these intervening two months, haven't there? I know you could list many.

In my own circle of friends and counselees, a number have suffered losses and reversals this spring. A teenager lost her mother in an auto accident. A mother lost her teenager in a freak home accident. In this same period, I've counseled with families who have lost others to suicide, abortion, cancer and AIDS. Mates have been abandoned without warning, children have run away, jobs have evaporated, diseases have struck. Even my own two children found themselves in the hospital as their college semesters entered the final weeks. Then last Saturday night, I found myself holding onto a friend as we stared into her blackened house where firefighters combed the debris for any lingering embers. Now it's Wednesday morning and I thought I had written the last sentence in this paragraph. But my secretary just told me that the sweet lady who sits right behind us in church every Sunday is in ICU. So, when I get back I'll try to make my point.

Well, hours have passed but I'm back. While I was in the ICU waiting room, word came of another church member in ER. And while I was in ER, I found out that our neighbor right across the street had been admitted with brain cancer. As I made my way back into my office, nursing thoughts of a locked door and a disconnected phone, I noticed on the shelf a gift from one of my 1980's stress management groups. It's a blue cap imprinted with orange and white letters that say, "Don't worry, be happy."

So what was that point I was leading up to almost 24 hours ago? Right now, it feels as the point is: don't ever write out a list of the trauma you have encountered over the past two months. It can be very depressing.

I began this revision on September 11, 2010, the ninth anniversary of the horrific attack on New York City's Twin Towers and on the Pentagon. As I reflect over the intervening years, the paragraphs above seem almost mild. It goes on, doesn't it? It goes on.

Our son, mentioned above, graduated and went right into the foreign mission field, only to return years later with disease that almost proved fatal. Our daughter and her husband are now across the Atlantic teaching at Cambridge University. A few months ago, doctors discovered that her appendix had ruptured—yet another call far too close, especially when we can't be right there with our children.

My father died in 1997 while the original edition of this book was with the publisher; my brother died unexpectedly in 2005; my mother joined them just this year, having lived to be 101.

I cannot begin to tell you the number of the funerals, hospitals visits and crisis counseling sessions. In my office last year, a friend tearfully confessed to murdering his wife fifteen years ago; I went with him as he turned himself in.

Floods struck our town; refugees moved into our church building. While hauling broken tree limbs I discovered that my Parkinson's, first diagnosed nearly four years ago, is, indeed, still slowly eating away at my physical and mental capacities. And that's just my little corner of the world. Hurricanes, tornados, revolutions and bloodshed in the Middle East, earthquakes, tsunamis, nuclear disasters—the axis of the earth has actually shifted beneath our feet.

It's the human condition, isn't it? It all brings us to a very simple point: You and I are vapor. All our plans are vapor. All our illusions of self-determination and control of our futures—vapor. We'd better get that straight and learn to pray *your will be done!* Anything else is madness. Whether insane delusion or insane despair, everything else is madness.

We have cried today. But we have rejoiced as well. Because there is a God. He is Father. He is in control. He is Savior. And *it is no longer I who live but Christ who lives in me!*

To pray *your will be done* is to unleash the one true power of prayer, for that power is God himself. To pray *your will be done* is to surround and saturate oneself with the omnipotence that holds the universe together, the cosmic force that brings order out of chaos. To pray *your will be done* is to gain freedom, freedom from self and all its impotence, ignorance and insecurity.

To pray *your will be done* is to escape the bonds of time, space and mortality and to seize upon eternity. I suppose that for God all of time and eternity must be one great *now,* the infinite instant. Nothing that is past, present or yet to come can fall outside the sovereignty of the God whose one moment is eternity. So to pray *your will be done* is to partake of eternity—to be enfolded and absorbed by the Eternal Almighty.

No wonder Jesus describes discipleship as a one-day-at-a-time affair. If all of his life is lived in the eternal now, when else could his disciples live? Yesterday is released to his mercy. Tomorrow is surrendered to his grace. Today we "seek first the kingdom."

Please don't read past that last sentence too quickly. It is drawn from the Sermon on the Mount where Jesus provides the antidote to worry.[152] Everyone says "don't worry," but everyone worries. And just saying "don't worry," isn't all that helpful, is it? If all I get from the Sermon is "don't worry," I'm not only likely to keep worrying, I'll probably worry about the fact that I'm worrying!

But Jesus doesn't stop with, "Don't worry." He gives the why and the how. Why not worry? Because the Father knows who you are and what you need. How not to worry? Refocus all that energy on a worthier target.

You see, Jesus never says, "Have no concern." Rather, he notes that some things are unworthy of a disciple's concern. How liberating it is to discover that concern—and therefore my ability to muster up massive quantities of it—isn't wrong in and of itself. In fact, it is a powerful dynamic, one of life's few constants! It doesn't have to be killed off. Rather, in Christ, I can tap that source of power for a worthy use, the Kingdom.

Jesus says that there is carnal concern and then there is Kingdom concern, crippling care and creative care.[153] And when I am absorbed enough in one, I have no room or energy left for the other. Jesus invites me to turn even my care and concern over to him for sanctification. He can transform fruitless, powerless, energy-sapping, common fretfulness into productive, potent, energizing, Kingdom consciousness.

Because it is Kingdom concern, this release from worry is not at all the same thing as carelessness. We're talking, not about devil-may-care foolishness, but God-does-care faithfulness. There is these days a popular pseudo-spirituality that apparently fails to make that distinction. The grace/faith nature of our discipleship is never an excuse for irresponsibility. I may sound pious when I qualify all my commitments with, "If the Lord wills." But there is no true piety there when I really mean, "If I fail to keep

---

152 Matthew 6:25-34.

153 The writer is indebted to Lloyd John Ogilvie for inspiring this sentence. In his book about the Sermon on the Mount, *A Life Full of Surprises* (Nashville: Abingdon Press, 1969, p. 111), he speaks of "creative anxiety" as the cure for neurotic anxiety.

this commitment, you can blame God!" Many misdeeds have been excused not only with, "The devil made me do it," but "The Lord led me to it."

Counselor types like to talk about something called "locus of control." If I claim an external locus of control, I see everyone and everything else as responsible for my life. I say things like, "Look what you made me do," and "I never get any breaks," and "Don't blame me—I was bottle fed and weaned too early!" If I claim an internal locus of control, I am taking responsibility for my own actions and reactions.

But what locus of control is the disciple to claim? If the core of my faith is self-denial/Christ-realization, doesn't that say that I no longer am in charge? And if I'm not in control, it follows that I'm not responsible, right? Over the last two millennia more than one heretic has gone down that road.

Instead, the disciple claims a third option, an eternal, heavenly locus of control. But as we discussed in the last chapter, heaven isn't far away and yet to come. In a very real and important sense it is here, now, and within.[154] This is a truth both liberating and obligating, both soothing and sobering. I no longer carry the weight of the world on my shoulders. I don't have to prove anything to God or anyone else.

At the same time, because it is no longer I but Christ, my sense of responsibility takes on new proportions. Whatever I do, I am called to do it with all my heart and soul because I do it "as to the Lord rather than to mortals."[155] From now on it's more than me, more than *my* reputation, more than *my* success or failure, more than *my* definition of excellence. For the ambassador of Christ, a lazy, slipshod carelessness is no longer an option. But neither is obsessiveness driven by guilt or pride.

Wearied and worn, I have come to the Master and accepted his invitation to rest. With that relief has come a new yoke and a fresh burden but they are the gentle yoke and the light burden of Jesus. So while I accept the responsibility and labor on, I do so with success guaranteed and with my soul at rest.[156]

Indwelt by the very Spirit of God, I am empowered to come at this matter of care from a whole new perspective. One of humanity's most

---

154 Luke 17:21.
155 Colossians 3:23.
156 Matthew 11:28-30. Colossians 3:23.

universally and deeply held assumptions is that one's inner state must necessarily and consistently reflect one's outer state. In other words, I'm conditioned to believe that I can be OK *in here* in my heart and mind only if things are OK *out there* in my world and relationships.

The ancient Stoics issued a rather extreme challenge to that assumption. They thought that the greatest attribute of God, and thus the greatest virtue of the godly, was the ability to be totally unaffected by life's ups and downs. The greatest good was a detachment that could say of the worst tragedies and losses, "I really don't care." The goal of Eastern religious meditation to produce "detachment" promotes the same idea: rise above all care.

Jesus, on the other hand, was *total* care, of those around him and of the will of his Father. He demonstrated a godliness so powerful that it could say, "I care passionately, but my care does not devastate me. I have a consistent inner contentment that is independent of outer circumstance. I rejoice with those who rejoice and weep with those who weep[157] but all the while it is well with my soul. I can undergo trial so severe, distress so acute, that my sweat turns bloody, and still I will maintain my sanity."

And apparently, Jesus can replicate that ability in a disciple. Paul told the Philippians that he had the inner sufficiency that the Stoics were always discussing. His circumstances could be favorable or brutal, and he could be content. "Not," he explained, "because I really don't care but because of the One who empowers me!"[158] The ultimate caring, Paul teaches us, is invoking the care of God in Christ.

Paul told the Corinthians that he was just "the clay pot." The circumstance-transcending power that fills the vessel isn't from self but from God alone. Immersed in *that* divine power, Paul said, even the most overwhelming circumstances needn't result in despair.[159]

For Paul, only one "circumstance" was the basis for his mental, emotional and spiritual state. It was the love of God which is in Christ Jesus and from which no external force in the universe can separate us![160]

According to most people, there is a law stating that there absolutely must be a direct cause/effect relationship between what happens to me

---

157 Romans 12:15.
158 Philippians 4:10-13.
159 II Corinthians 4:7-9.
160 Romans 8:38, 39.

Faith Not only in Christ
but also of Christ
You surrender to the Christ in you.

externally and how I respond internally. But according to Paul, in Christ, that law, too, has been rescinded! So why do I still act as if that law were immutable? Am I afraid that if I don't get sufficiently crazy, folks won't know just how *bad* things really are? If I don't fall to pieces, will they think that I'm saying that everything is OK? Do I somehow believe that certain calamities are so catastrophic that they require madness? Will injustice result if I don't break down?

But then I look at Jesus: never indifferent or aloof; always passionately, vulnerably engaged in the human situation; yet never once sent into an emotional tailspin—in himself, always OK! No one has ever had more right to be out of control or out of commission with anger, frustration, consternation and grief over the way people act and the way things go. But there he stands, always caring but never crazy, even wounded but not worried. It's as if he doesn't even know about that unbreakable, inescapable control tether that allows every outward event to jerk and tug directly upon inward well-being. It's as if he knows of a stronger cable, one that connects the heart directly to the peace of God.

What we are talking about is sanity, not simple-mindedness—wellness of soul, not absence of agony.

Look again at Luke 22:43, 44, another one of those peculiar scriptural sequences. I want the passage to say that the agony increased to the point of bloodsweat, then the praying intensified, and then the angel strengthened him. After that, of course, there should be no more agony, no sweat. But that isn't the way it reads, is it? Maybe Luke is telling us that God's strengthening isn't meant to shelter us from all trial, but to prepare us for and preserve us through it.

> *Oh for a faith that will not shrink, though pressed by ev'ry foe,*
> *That will not tremble on the brink of any earthly woe.*
> *That will not murmur or complain beneath the chast'ning rod,*
> *But in the hour of grief or pain will lean upon its God.*
> *A faith that shines more bright and clear when tempests rage without*
> *That when in danger knows no fear, in darkness feels no doubt![161]*

---

161 Bathurst, William H., *O For a Faith that will not Shrink.*

Gal. 2:20
one more time

I Live no more!

But who has such a faith? Isn't it ridiculous to speak of Jesus in the garden as if that has any application to a weak, pitiful waverer like me? The God-cable may control his response but the world-tether is still very much connected to mine. O for *the* faith of Christ himself!

But then I am brought back one more time to our title passage, Galatians 2:20. In the first rendering of it in Chapter One, you may have caught that odd-sounding construction, *in faith of the Son of God* where other translations read *by faith in the Son of God*? Paul uses a word that ordinarily would be rendered "of" rather than "in."[162] There are times when Paul literally talks of faith *in* Christ,[163] just as here he talks literally about a faith *of* Christ.

Perhaps, as many scholars would argue, Paul uses the words interchangeably. But what if in Galatians 2:20 and similar passages, he is saying something else? Even if he isn't excluding the idea of faith *in*, could he be saying something more? Could he be talking about the very faith *of* Jesus himself and the absorption of our faith into his? Could he be saying that there really is just one saving faith, the faith that Jesus lived out in perfect obedience to the Father? Is he saying that by grace we can take this Christ-faith as our own?

Just a few verses back, in Galatians 2:16, Paul also speaks first of justification through faith (literally) "*of* Christ Jesus" so that then we who have believed (literally) "*in* Christ Jesus" might, indeed, be justified by faith (literally) "*of* Christ." *Faith of, faith in, faith of.* More than inspired redundancy, this may be Paul's way of saying that the saving faith to which we resign our own faith is the justified and justifying faith of Jesus Christ.

So if you and I were to ask Paul if this redeeming Christ-faith is the faith *in* Christ or the faith *of* Christ, he might just say, "Yes!"

Lord, give us such a faith as this; and then whate'er may come,
We'll taste e'en here the hallowed bliss of an eternal home.[164]

What a glorious thought: "E'en here," he takes our mustard seed faith and plunges it into his mountain moving faith![165] To speak, then, of our faith is to speak of Jesus' faith, the faith that prays, "Your will be done."

162 See also Romans 3:22-26; Galatians 3:22; and Philippians 3:9.
163 See Galatians 3:26; Colossians 1:4, 2:5; I Timothy 3:13; and II Timothy 3:15.
164 Bathurst.
165 Matthew 17:20.

There's a tale of a barnyard of geese that gathered each week to hear their eldest repeat the story of the Great White Gander who, long ago, spread his magnificent wings and flew over the barnyard fence to freedom. The story was well told and so inspiring that all the geese would honk their approval and sometimes even flap wings of excitement. Each week they would repeat this ritual because it was a very important part of their lives. But, oddly enough, it never occurred to any of them to spread their own wings and fly![166]

I've been told that you can put a flea in an empty mayonnaise jar and screw on the lid. Intelligent creature that he is, the flea will soon learn not to jump so high as to keep hitting the lid. But even more industrious than he is intelligent, the flea will keep jumping in a useless kind of "freedom gesture." Once he is sufficiently conditioned, you can remove the lid and that flea will continue to jump just short of the jar's top. Parade past the jar your dog, your cat or your kids; the flea will just keep jumping at a fraction of his capacity, just short of freedom. He'll jump until exhaustion beats him and he dies.

I'd like to think of myself as somewhat brighter than geese or fleas. But how much of my life is spent in "freedom gesture" jumping? "Honk if you love Jesus!" I do that. I even flap about it sometimes. But how often have I actually spread my own wings and flown with Christ?

As a child did you ever feel invincible? Do you remember when you thought you could fly? How many bumps and bruises, grouches and grown-ups, slip ups and sins did it take for you to realize that your wings were clipped? When did you first know, without a doubt, that you were in a fairly small jar with a very tight lid?

But wait. Listen... Whose voice is that?

...you will know the truth and the truth will set you free![167]

We're just awfully conditioned, aren't we, by the past with all its limitation and pain and failure? It's one thing to talk about self-denial/ Christ-realization, to speak of a Christ-faith without limits. It's quite another to really decide to jump—this time all the way to the freedom that Christ promises—only to see again that greasy lid zooming at us with

---

166 Adapted from the parable by Søren Kierkegaard recorded in Walter Lowrie, *A Short Life of Kierkegaard*, Princeton, Princeton Press, 1942, pp. 235-237.

167 John 8:32.

horrifying speed. I remember how much that collision hurts, don't you? Anyway, people seem happy enough with our industrious gesture-jumping. Just today, someone complimented one of my little leaps; how about you? Real jumping can be dangerous; people who try to fly are taken away and locked up. We'd do well just to sit here and talk the radical talk about the big jump and the faith flight. We can theologize and theorize about the restoration of sin-clipped wings. Maybe I *will* write another chapter or two on how it might be if only there were no lids, if only we had the power...

...if the Son sets you free, you will be free indeed![168]

Is that voice getting louder? Is it just me, or do you feel some direct Sonlight on your head? Where could it be coming from? Look up—that's not a lid! It's much too blue; it's far too clear...

> *Look, I have set before you an open door that no one can shut;*
> *for though you have but little power of your own, you still*
> *have kept my word and have not denied my name.*
>
> *Revelation 3:8b*

It's true: I do have but little power. Isn't that the problem? More than the lid, I fear the open sky. I don't have the power—my eyes are too weak to take in the blue brilliance; my lungs can't tolerate the pure, bracing air; my limbs are too feeble to propel me through the boundless expanse. Sometimes I feel like a prisoner released after thirty years into a frighteningly alien world. He's overwhelmed; he doesn't know how to be free. To his own horror, he finds himself actually longing for the secure familiarity of prison. What's the saying, "better a known evil than an unknown good"?

I once had a counselee who had been so severely abused through most of her life that when I asked her to tell me about joy, her only response was a vacant stare. I tried to prompt her, "A time you experienced some joy... A way you might yet experience joy..." Finally, she spoke. Subdued, but matter-of-fact. Subtly bemused. Too soulless even to register despair. "That's not for me."

Like an untouchable in a rigid caste system, she knew that having joy was no more a part of her life script than being a princess or a priest. She

---

168 John 8:36.

just couldn't process joy. Virtually every significant power and authority figure in the first 16 years of her life had driven the message deep into her psyche, "Work is for you, fear is for you, abuse is for you, but joy is not for you."

I wanted to take her hand and say, "Joy is most especially for you. The joy of Christ is for you, of all people! In him you *are* royalty; you *are* a priest. His joy was meant for *you!*"

Profoundly saddened and frustrated for her, I struggled long and hard to assist her in her healing. At times I even grew impatient. Why did she continue to believe the lies? Why couldn't she see who she really was? And now here I sit, at then end of this book, slapped in the face with the fact that I am far more like her than I have ever grasped or admitted. Faith in such joy comes and goes, I'm afraid.

I may be smarter than the goose or the flea but that only means that I can conjure up more frightening scenarios to keep me earthbound. How clever I can be at disguising a faint heart as a discrete mind, faithlessness as level-headedness, worried equivocation as wise deliberation. Who in the world am I to launch out, to reach out, to embrace the outrageous extravagance of God's love? My life script says that I am to be just a good, respectable, congenial, *safe* Christian. Of course, someone like Peter could jump out of the boat and walk on water. But then even Peter looked away from Jesus and down at the waves. And even Peter then began to sink into those waves. Yes, I know Jesus caught him but why should he catch me?

Take courage! It is I. Do not be afraid![169]

Afraid? Of course I'm afraid. I know that voice. It's the same Voice that called me Adversary: "Get out of my way, *Satan!*" The words still cut like a knife; still they wound my pride and slash my progress... What progress? For all my effort, I haven't been able to come any closer to heaven. Each fresh failure follows me, clamoring, "Satan!"

Now suddenly, silence.

Then, into that gaping wound flows a soothing balm of *healing* words from Jesus: "Deny...take up...follow." And a cross appears before me. As I catch the crossbeam, I am lifted up to see my Savior standing on the shimmer of sea, holding his hand out to me.

---

169 Matthew 14:27b.

Lord, if it is you, tell me to come to you...[170] Let your perfect love cast out fear[171] and pull me away from mere safety. Take me wherever, do with me whatever. Just let me be with you; let it all be you. It doesn't matter where or how or what I do to serve you; it's all you. If I falter you *will* catch me, just because of who you are. *Lord, if it's you, tell me to come to you...*

"Come."[172]

Yes, I do know that Voice, now so full of grace and glory. It *is* he and he wants me. He has come all this way, has stridden the waves of the cosmos to seek and save... me. Me!

And now has all the dead weight of my sin fallen away? Is this cross a buoy? I don't know; I can see only Jesus. Jesus ablaze with a love that enraptures me, captures me, fixes my gaze on his face and attunes my ear to his call. I don't even notice that the swirling foam is now somehow my solid footing.

Thank you, Lord. Thank you for words that pierce and words that heal. Thank you for unlidded jars, wide open doors and unmanned boats. Thank you for wings spread wide and lifted high upon your Spirit-wind. Now take me, make me water-walker, cloud-dancer, heaven-ladder. Live in me, Lord. Let me live in you. No longer I but I-in-you.

No longer I but Christ in me.

And the secret is simply this: Christ in you! Yes, Christ in you bringing with him the hope of all the glorious things to come.[173]

Yes, Lord. Come!

Read this again
and again
and then
again.

---

170 Matthew 14:28.
171 I John 4:18.
172 Matthew 14:29.
173 Colossians 1:27b (Phillips).

No Longer I

Study Guide

This companion to the book, *No Longer I*, is designed to help you derive the greatest benefit from your reading. You can use this study guide in your own personal study, for small group discussion, or for a larger class. The book's thirteen chapters easily enable a three month study. Depending on the people involved, the material can support a six month treatment as well. Another workable approach is organized around the book's five major sections of two and three chapters each. Group members can read a section a week, discussing the highlights that most interest them, completing the study in five or six weeks.

First, let us briefly introduce you to the SAPE Bible study system. The SAPE system involves a four step approach to Bible study.

- First you *Summarize* a passage with an abbreviated paraphrase.
- Then you *Analyze* it using whatever study tools are available to help you interpret the passage in greater depth.
- Next you *Personalize* the passage. Where are you in the narrative? How is God wanting you to apply this scripture to your own life?
- Finally, you *Evangelize* the text. That is, you look for the good news imbedded in it that you can pass on to others in word or deed.

You may wish to use this system in your own study of the key biblical passages cited in *No Longer I*. You can use a similar approach in your study of the book itself. With each chapter, summarize for yourself its main points, then look for further implications and applications. Ask yourself where you fit in the chapter; what does it have to say to your own life? Then, what can you take with you from the chapter that will help your life be a more effective testimony for Jesus to others?

Similarly, this study guide provides not only a set of questions for each chapter but space to write out four kinds of personal responses to the chapter. These are titled *Thoughts, Feelings, Questions* and *So What?*

Thoughts: What new insights did I gain from the chapter? What, to me, are the most important ideas it touches? Why? What lines of further thinking does it suggest? If I were to write a follow-up chapter, what would I include?

Feelings: What emotions did I experience in the reading? Which portions resonated most for me? What are these feelings telling me about myself?

Questions: What questions did the chapter raise for me? What portions did I find unclear or confusing? What new questions does the chapter suggest for me to explore?

So What? Where to from here? What difference will reading this chapter make in my faith walk? What do I want to do about it?

Finally, we want to encourage you to make this study an ongoing dialogue with the Lord. Carefully consider all the Biblical passages cited in *No Longer I.* Read from your own Bible not only the scriptures that are quoted but those listed in the footnotes. And bathe this study in prayer. Begin and end each reading and each use of this guide by offering it up to God and by asking for his will to be done. Let the study be less your doing and more a work of God in your life.

Why not begin with prayer right now? Share with God what you want to experience in this study. What outcome will make it a success for you? Ask him to help you realize the results he has in mind for you. Then use the rest of this page to write out your goals for this study, what you believe to be God's will for you as you journey into the depths of Matthew 16:24 and Galatians 2:20. May he bless you richly!

PART ONE
THE CROSS OF CHRIST

Before reading Part One, consider the following questions.

1) Do you have a favorite saying? Is there a statement you make so often that people associate its wording especially with you?

2) What would you say is the signature statement of Jesus, the one sentence that best represents Jesus' message to his disciples?

3) How would you define self-denial? How have you denied yourself?

4) What struggles do you have with this matter of self-denial?

5) How would you paraphrase Galatians 2:20? If someone totally unfamiliar with the passage asked you what it was getting at, how would you reply?

PROLOGUE

1) Why do you suppose Jesus chose the region of Caesarea Philippi to ask the disciples, "Who do you say I am?"

2) How do suppose Peter felt when he was the first to answer, "...Messiah, Son of the Living God!"? And how would you have felt to hear Jesus' response of blessing? What would you have made of it when Jesus called you Peter (Rock) rather than Simon?

3) Then how was Jesus able to go so quickly from calling Peter "blessed" to calling him "Satan"? How do you think you might have responded to Jesus at that point?

4) What to you are the most vital points of Matthew 16:13-23? With what questions does the story leave you?

ONE: "...WHO LOSE THEIR LIFE FOR MY SAKE"

1) How does this chapter's definition of self-denial differ from others you have heard?

2) Christians are called to bear their cross. What does that mean to you? What are some other meanings you have heard?

3) How would you describe the relationship between Matthew 16:24 and Galatians 2:20?

4) Which pet vices or self-indulgences are hard for you to surrender? Which spiritual virtues and achievements are sources of pride for you? Which "garbage" is harder for you to throw out, your offenses or your attainments?

5) How would you explain self-denial/Christ-realization to a friend? Do you like the phrase self-forgetting/Christ-absorption better? What other phrasing could be used?

Thoughts

Feelings

Questions

So What?

TWO: "...THE SCANDAL OF THE CROSS..."

1) Complete this sentence: When I consider the Cross of Christ...

2) How has the Cross become so sterilized and pretty? To you, how is the true beauty of the Cross different from mere prettiness?

3) Who should be scandalized by the Cross? Why?

4) How is God glorified in something so shameful as a criminal's torturous execution?

5) What thoughts and feelings were sparked when you read, "You are Barabbas"? How are you similar to Barabbas? How are you different?

6) If the Cross of Christ truly is our cross, then how do we become scandals—stumbling blocks—to the world?

Thoughts

Feelings

Questions

So What?

PART TWO
THE MIND OF CHRIST

Before reading Part Two, consider the following questions.

1) Self-denial, self-contempt and self-acceptance—in your opinion how do these three differ or compare? How do they relate to each other?

2) Where would you plot your opinion on this spectrum?

"Self-esteem is /----------------------/---------------------/ "Self esteem is
essential to mental   humanistic sin that
and spiritual wholeness."   fulfills II Timothy 3:2."

3) Where would you plot your opinion on this next spectrum?

"Self-denial and self-acceptance are mutually exclusive."
Totally True /--------------------------/------------------------/ Totally False

4) How strongly do you agree or disagree with this statement about acts of faith and service?

"If you do it without really feeling it, you're being a hypocrite."
Fully Agree /--------/------------/--------+--------/ Completely Disagree

Essential Paradox
Self denial is the one path
to legitmate self-acceptance,

Weaknesses
Strength

Joyful Pain
My Savior

Christian
At the Heart of Self-Denial
is a beneficial forgetfullness,
not a cripling self-contempt.

How many times do we make God
the means to other Ends.   Could we Love God
without His gifts.

THREE: "AREN'T YOU WORTH MUCH MORE...

1) Who do you agree or sympathize with most in the opening story, Isaac Watts ("...such a worm as I...") or the farmhand ("I ain't no worm!") Why?

2) How do you understand Paul's reference to "lovers of self" in II Tim. 3:2?

3) The psychological and the spiritual—how do you think these "two distinct but overlapping areas" relate to each other?

4) What is "the essential paradox" discussed in this chapter? How do you understand it and apply it to yourself?

5) Can you think of specific examples of "finding through losing?"

6) What are some of the ways we try to hire Jesus as an assistant rather than surrender to him as Lord and Savior?

Thoughts

Feelings

Questions

So What?

FOUR: "...SET YOUR MIND..."

1) See how many different sources of motivation you can think of for your different behaviors and thoughts. Is there one kind of motivation that seems to predominate? Would you say that it is an Infant (Feeling), Child (Approval), or Adult (Conscience) level motivation?

2) When are you most likely to do something without realizing why? Do you recall the last time you heard yourself say, "What was I thinking?"

3) How would you describe the concept of conscience to someone who was unfamiliar with the word? To you, what are the important distinctions of the *Christ-Centered* Conscience; how does it differ from the conscience of a noble unbeliever?

4) "The conscience must say that the conscience must rule." How is the conscience able to "turn itself on," independent of circumstance or stimulus?

Thoughts

Feelings

Questions

So What?

FIVE: "...TRANSFORMED BY RENEWAL OF THE MIND"

1) For you, what is the most important difference between joy and happiness, as the terms are used in this chapter?

2) Recall an event which was, for you, a major deposit in the Bank of Acceptance. Recall a time when you realized that you had made a costly withdrawal.

3) Have you ever struggled with self-forgiveness? What exactly do you think is involved in forgiving yourself?

4) When you perform an act of self-sacrifice without "feeling like it," do you consider yourself a hypocrite? Why or why not?

5) Describe from your own life a time when the old Image-Habit-Action-Attitude chain seemed to have you defeated. How was the "missing link" provided? How is the old Image reformed?

Thoughts

Feelings

Questions

So What?

PART THREE
THE BODY OF CHRIST

Before reading Part Three, consider the following questions.

1) Name the biggest celebrity you know personally.

2) The church is a body, a family, a priesthood, a kingdom, a temple. What do each of these mean to you? Which is your favorite? Why?

3) Are you able to feel closer to God through private devotion or through corporate worship? Why? What benefit is unique to each?

4) When you hear the word "fellowship," what images come to mind? If someone were to ask you to write a short paragraph on Christian fellowship, what would you write?

5) Describe what would be for you the perfect worship service.

6) Is there anything in worship that really annoys you? The song selection? The preacher's speaking style? Mannerisms of a prayer leader? Activities for which you see no purpose? How might these distractions for you be aids for someone else to worship more wholeheartedly?

SIX: "...TO THE LEAST OF THESE..."

1) Some Christians make it easy for us to see Christ in them; others make it hard. Describe someone you know in the first group. What most blocks your view of Christ in others? What would help you to see past that obstruction?

2) Practically speaking, what difference does second-person self-denial/ Christ-realization make? How will it show itself in the way we treat each other?

3) What does corporate self-denial/Christ-realization mean to you? Again, practically how does a surrendered church look?

4) One model of church growth suggests that a church should target a specific population so that most members will share the same socio-economic and cultural background. What, to you, are the strengths and weaknesses of this model in light of second-person and corporate self-denial/Christ-realization?

5) Reflecting on first-person, second-person, and corporate self-denial/ Christ-realization, what would you say in a paragraph titled, *Christ is all and in all*?

Thoughts

Feelings

Questions

So What?

SEVEN: "...DISTINGUISHING THE BODY..."

1) Describe what was for you a truly meaningful worship assembly.

2) What helps you to maximize the worship experience? What tends to hinder meaningful worship for you?

3) If you were a worship leader sincerely concerned about "cruciform worship" that glorifies God and edifies the body, how would go about the specifics of planning and evaluating worship experiences?

4) What memories, emotions and ideas do you connect with the word "communion?"

5) How would you paraphrase I Corinthians 11:23-32?

6) Respond to the book's statement that the Lord's Supper "may be the consummate expression of the nature of the Christian assembly."

Thoughts

Feelings

Questions

So What?

PART FOUR
THE WORD OF CHRIST

Before reading Part Four, consider the following questions.

1) What might self-denial/Christ-realization have to do with the way a believer interacts with an unbeliever?

2) What is the first thing that comes to your mind when you hear the word *evangelism?*

3) In this section, we will be looking at such matters as truth, absolutes, moral codes and values. How do you think these relate to self-denial/Christ-realization?

4) What is truth? Looking through the lens provided in Galatians 2:20, how are we better able to see truth?

5) Jesus said that divine law could be summed up in love for God and others. What does that mean to you? How does such an ethical system look, one based on Biblical love?

EIGHT: "...IF THEY KEPT QUIET..."

1) What is the most outrageous thing you've heard or seen a preacher do during a sermon to get his point across?

2) What are some important but "heard-too-often, known-too-well" sermon topics that you tend to tune out unless they are presented in unusual ways?

3) What do you think people were expecting from Jesus as they shouted, "Hosanna!"? What kind of deliverance were they looking for? What for you really is at the heart of deliverance?

4) In recent years, the word "evangelist" has received a lot of bad press. What can be done to restore the definition of evangelism as "telling the good news" rather than "bad news"? How do you feel about being an evangelist, a teller of good news?

5) How does the concept of self-denial/Christ-realization change your perspective of unbelievers and of yourself as Christ's ambassador?

Thoughts

Feelings

Questions

So What?

NINE: "...A WAY THAT SEEMS RIGHT..."

1) Consider the following spectrums, plotting on each yourself and your opinion about truth.

Larry B.O. Hol Nov. 2

Truth is   A 30   Truth is *Christ God*
Precept /----------------- P 40 -------/----------------------------/ Person

Truth is   A 40   Truth is
Fluid   /----------------- P40 -------/----------------------------/ Fixed

Truth is Wholly   30 A   Truth is Wholly
Knowable /----------- 30 P --------/----------------------/ Unknowable

2) What do you think of the statement that God's truth may be suprarational (more than rational) but never irrational (less than rational)?

3) We all tend to make truth subject to something--our traditions, emotions, rational processes, etc. To what are you most likely to make truth subject?

Jesus - Absolute

Thoughts

Feelings

Questions

So What?

Best Possible Life!

164

Every Conceivable Thing
Non-Exsitant
or Being
Exists
Impossible
contingent
necessary

TEN: "IF YOU LOVE ME..."

1) In your opinion, what did the Love Generation get right? Where did they go wrong?

2) Antinomianism (no law) and Pharisaism (all law) both can be attractive. What do you find appealing about each? To which do you feel most drawn? Which do you see as the greater problem in today's society, in the church?

3) How do you see all "human-isms" going back to the fall of Adam and Eve?

4) What to you are the strengths and weaknesses of situation ethics?

5) How do we decide when we do not have a direct "thus saith the Lord"? What do you do when all your choices seem only to be between lesser evils?

6) What to you is the difference between doing the right thing because it works best for all involved, and doing it because it is God's will?

Thoughts

Feelings

Questions

So What?

PART FIVE
THE FAITH OF CHRIST

Before reading Part Five, consider the following questions.

1) What does it mean to be born again? How does it happen?

2) Describe your own conversion experience. What is your most vivid memory of it?

3) When do you feel most centered, congruous, in synch and in tune? When do you most feel a sense of clashing disharmony, at odds with yourself and with everything else?

4) What do you see as the big difference between healthy spiritual simplicity and unhealthy spiritual simplism?

5) When have you felt the most overwhelmed? What did you do?

6) What is the most common theme in your personal prayers?

7) How would you describe Christian faith to a seeker?

8) Where would you plot your position between these two statements?
Christians should be   Christians should be
the most /-------------------------------/---------------------------/ the most
careful people.   carefree people.

ELEVEN: "...BORN AGAIN"

1) Name some of the most significant or even radical changes you have made in your life.

2) How would you describe the idea of conversion to someone who was unfamiliar with the term?

3) Reread John 3, putting yourself in Nicodemus' place. How well do you think you would have understood Jesus? What would you have made of his call to be born of water and Spirit?

4) There are so many different ideas and practices surrounding baptism that it can be confusing and frustrating; it's tempting just to avoid the subject altogether. But the New Testament has a number of important things to say about baptism, so it must be worthy of study. What are some of the things you have heard about baptism? If you had to write a paragraph summarizing just what the Bible says about baptism, what would you write? Would you emphasize method or meaning? How are the two related?

Thoughts

Feelings

Questions

So What?

TWELVE: "...SEATED...IN THE HEAVENLIES..."

1) What would you say is the worst color combination? How about the worst flavor combination?

2) In your faith walk, where are you on these spectrums?

Total /---------------------------------/-------------------------/ Total
Congruity   Incongruity

"I don't even /---------------------------------/-----------------------/ "There is now
know what I'm doing!"   no condemnation!"

3) What does it mean to you to be *co-seated in the heavenlies in Christ Jesus*? What do you understand that to mean? What do you feel about it?

4) What are some "self-ish" ways we try to resolve the spiritual dissonance in our lives? What "counterfeit congruity" is most tempting for you? Why?

Thoughts

Feelings

Questions

So What?

Healthy Spiritual
Simplicity
or Unhealthy
Spiritual Simplism

In view of Eternit,
Simple Reality
of the Granduer
of God.

THIRTEEN: "...YOUR WILL BE DONE"

1) What can give you feelings of real panic or profound dread? At such times, what are you most likely to pray for? What is the most difficult thing about praying, "Not my will, but yours?" How does that prayer help?

2) When is it easiest to remember that you are *vapor*? When is it hardest?

3) Tell of a time when Kingdom concern crowded out your carnal concern.

4) What does it mean to you to have a faith *in* Christ that is, in fact, the faith *of* Christ? What difference does that word "of" really make? How does it change the practice of living by faith?

5) What has made you feel like the lid was still on the jar? Which of the tempter's lies formerly kept you comfortable with mere "gesture jumping"? Seeing now that the lid is removed, what do you want to do? What will Christ in you do?

Thoughts

Feelings

Questions

So What?

Jan. 4, 12
new wed.
Classes

P. S. WHERE TO FROM HERE?

1) We've covered a lot of territory together, haven't we? This may be a good time to go back and reread some chapters of *No Longer I*. Portions that may have been difficult at first can now be clarified by the rest of the book. Which chapters were the hardest for you?

2) Look back over your answers in this study guide, too. If you were to give those answers now, which ones would differ most from your original responses? Why?

3) What changes are you aware of that *Christ in you* is already achieving, even since you began this study?

4) Sometimes, after an intensive study like this, the Holy Spirit makes his truths sink in deeper and then resurface over time in more fully owned thoughts and behaviors. Then the study can be re-experienced at a whole new level. If you were to repeat this study, how long would you want to wait first? What would you do differently this time?

5) Regardless of how often you revisit *No Longer I*, you always want to stay in God's word. Which Bible passages have become especially significant to you during this study? Which of those would you like to study now using the SAPE system (see the introduction of this study guide)? Which passages do you want to memorize?

6) If you were to use the SAPE system to study one of the four accounts of the Gospel next, would you choose Matthew, Mark, Luke or John? Why?

7) Of course, you also want to stay in prayer, claiming God's promises in Christ and relying on the Spirit's intercession. What changes do you anticipate in your prayer live now?

8) What do you think the Lord is ready to do in your life now in the areas of Christian service, fellowship and worship?

9) What other books or studies would you like to move into from here?

10) If you were to write the sequel to *No Longer I* ,what would you say? Which topics would you cover in greater depth? What new areas would you explore? Remember, Christ *is* writing his story in you. Expect him to be at work in your study, your prayers and in your church and daily life, showing you more and more the glorious truth that it really is no longer you but Christ who lives in you! May God richly bless you in this the greatest adventure of all!

John 17

CPSIA information can be obtained at www.ICGtesting.com
Printed in the USA
240329LV00001B/3/P

Riches from Our Earth

by C. Truman Rogers

Scott Foresman
is an imprint of

Glenview, Illinois • Boston, Massachusetts • Chandler, Arizona
Upper Saddle River, New Jersey

ISBN 13: 978-0-328-52676-5
ISBN 10:　　0-328-52676-2

3 4 5 6 7　V0N4　17 16 15 14 13 12 11 10

Not Just Rocks

People have used rock in many ways since ancient times. Among the earliest shelters for humans were rock caves. During the Stone Age, people used rock to make their tools and art.

Rocks come in many colors. The walls of the Grand Canyon, which are made of layers of many kinds of rock, are striped in colors from gray to brownish red. At sunset, the canyon walls seem to glow, the colors changing from purplish to fiery red. Some rocks look almost black, and some look almost white.

Rocks are made of
minerals. Scientists study
minerals. Their research
helps them understand
how our planet was made
and how it is changing.